Paperback Fantastic issue one
Published April 2022

Edited
by Justin Marriott (thepaperbackfanatic@sky.com)

Cover designed
by Bill Cunningham (cinexploits@gmail.com)
Image taken from Catherine Jeffrey Jones art for the Ace edition of *Sargasso of Space* by Andre Norton
Frontispiece from Ed Emshwiller art for Lancer edition of *The Currents of Space* by Isaac Asimov
All art and images reproduced purely for the purposes of historical context and no copyright infringement intended

Contributors
Tim Deforest
Andreas Decker
Dave Karlen
John Peel
Jeff Popple
Scott Ranalli
Penny Tesarek
Tom Tesarek
Benjamin Thomas

Dedicated to
Tom Tesarek - whose suggestions, editing, proofing and scans make this a much better publication

THE PAPERBACK FANTASTIC

FANTASTIC

VOLUME 1:

SCIENCE FICTION

LISTING OF REVIEWS

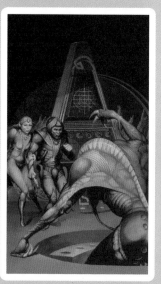

FANTASTIC FACTOIDS

ACE DOUBLE:
INVADERS FROM EARTH
ACROSS TIME
Robert Silverberg/David Grinnell (Donald A. Wollheim)
1958

"Innovative and inventive SF yarn..."

Invaders From Earth is an innovative and inventive SF yarn from the then-rising star Robert Silverberg. A public relations man gets creative when humanity discovers intelligent life on Ganymede, but they're standing in the way of corporate profits. He invents a colony on the moon and plans a "massacre" that will allow humans to wipe out the natives. Slowly, though, he becomes aware of the evil in his actions. A nice, unusual story of awakening from a real professional. The other half of the book is a let-down. This time, the story reads like it's from a Thirties' pulp magazine. Three human beings are snatched from our time and taken a million years into the future. They discover that humankind has evolved into energy beings, but that they're obviously still human – they're still at war. The ideas are sound enough, but the story grinds to a halt constantly as the writer gives you page after page of exposition. And his attempts at realism in his characters just doesn't ring true. Two brothers who dislike one another for contrived reasons are (gasp!) in love with the same girl. She marries one, but has she made a mistake? Who cares?
John Peel

INVADERS �֎ ✶ ✶ ✶
ACROSS ✶ ✶

ACE DOUBLE:
THE SPACE WILLIES
SIX WORLDS YONDER
Eric Frank Russell
1958

"Extremely irreverent and enjoys demolishing clay idols ..."

There's no downside to this Double since both are by Russell, one of the best writers of the period. *The Space Willies* (published in England as *Next of Kin*) is a hysterical story about an interplanetary war against the "Combine". John Leeming becomes a prisoner of war, and you might think that the rest of the tale would be about him trying to escape – but

it isn't. It's about how he wins the war while remaining a prisoner... (Russell would do something vaguely similar with another brilliant novel, *Wasp*.) Russell loved to author stories about misunderstandings between humans and aliens and the consequences – usually to the detriment of the aliens. Another example is included in *Six Worlds Yonder*: the very funny 'Diabologic'. *Six Worlds Yonder* is (unsurprisingly) a collection of six of Russell's best short stories and show off his feverish imagination and way with words and wit. He's extremely irreverent and enjoys demolishing clay idols and does it with skill and great dollops of fun. You'll love both.
John Peel

✶ ✶ ✶ ✶ ✶

ACE DOUBLE:
ALPHA YES, TERRA NO!
THE BALLAD OF BETA-2
Emil Petaja/Samuel R. Delaney
1965

"Tries an experimental approach that almost pays off...."

In *Alpha Yes*, humanity is looking to the stars for living room, and the inhabitants of Alpha Centauri don't like what they see. An agent of theirs comes to the Earth – a shapeshifter, who changes his face, form and species at will. He has a plan – but is it to save Earth of to condemn it? An interesting story that will keep you guessing, though the ending falls a little flat. Petaja has an interesting way with words, and a decided

THE SPACE WILLIES
An uncredited cover depicting the capture of John Leeming, a maverick and rebellious soldier, who gives his captors the "willies".

ACROSS TIME
A cut down version of a 1957 hardback formed half of this Ace Double. Cover uncredited but assumed to be by Ed Valigursky

THE BALLAD OF BETA -2
A slim novel weighing at 96 pages, with an equally slim pay-off. Cover art by Jack Gaughan.

ACE
DOUBLE NOVEL
BOOKS

TWO COMPLETE NOVELS 35c

D-315   You can't keep an Earthman down

THE SPACE WILLIES

ERIC
FRANK
RUSSELL
Complete & Unabridged

ace
DOUBLE NOVEL
BOOKS

TWO COMPLETE NOVELS 35c

D-286

Kidnapped into the future!

ACROSS TIME

David Grinnell
Complete and Unabridged

ace
double

M-121 45¢

Between the distant stars lay terror

THE BALLAD OF BETA-2

Samuel R. Delany

Complete Novel

viewpoint on the poor direction humanity is taking. Samuel R. Delaney would go on to author award-winning novels, but *The Ballard of Beta-2* was one of his early works where he's still trying to find his footing. It's an unusual tale in which a jaded student must try some literary criticism on the title song. He investigates it and finds that it's not as cut and dried as he first assumed. As with a lot of Delaney's work, this is unusual and a different sort of a book than you might expect. The story could have been told in a simpler fashion as a straight narrative, but instead he tries an experimental approach that almost pays off. But only almost. In the end, you're left thinking "is that it?"
John Peel

ALPHA ⚛⚛⚛
BALLAD ⚛⚛⚛

ACE DOUBLE:
THE ARSENAL OF MIRACLES
ENDLESS ESCAPE
Gardner F. Fox/John Brunner
1964

"This is too much fun; we'd better dull it up…"

Arsenal - Bran Magannon was an Admiral of the Earth Empire before he fell in love with Queen Peganna of the Lyanir and defeated their battle fleet – and lost Peganna. Now he wanders from world to world, Bran the Wanderer, Bran the Lucky. But Peganna has tracked him down and asks his help in finding a new home for her dying people. Together, they must discover the mysteries of the long dead Crenn Lir and discover why it is that Peganna's people are dying. Fox is probably best known these days for his long run on the old **Justice League of America** comics, but – even while he was writing them – he was also well known for his SF novels. This one, merges SF and Fantasy in a joyful romp that show his writing skills off to the full.

Endless - The editor must have looked at the first half of this book and said: "This is too much fun; we'd better dull it up." So, he picked a short John Brunner novel (a writer who never seemed to me to have the slightest idea of what fun was) to take the edge off. It's hard to summarize the story because I can't make any sense out of it. In the far future, humanity has spread out to some forty-odd worlds using spaceships, but now

they have developed the technology to build Bridges to connect these worlds instantly. One world decides it doesn't want to join up, and various characters have mental breakdowns and/or suicidal tendencies as a result. It's really not worth trying to make sense out of this.
John Peel

ARSENAL ⚛⚛⚛⚛
ENDLESS ⚛

ACE DOUBLE:
GHOST BREAKER
CLOCKWORK'S PIRATES
Ron Goulart
1971

"More like notes for stories than actual stories…"

Goulart is a bit of an acquired taste. His stories are all filled with silliness and illogic, and most of them have malfunctioning robots and/or androids in them. *Clockwork's Pirates* is a typical example – mechanical pirates have kidnapped the daughter of a regional governor on an alien world. Special agent John Wesley Sand is sent to retrieve her (hopefully with her virtue and life both intact) against many bizarre foes. Lots of goofy fun ensues. *Ghost Breaker* (I'll bet he wished he'd called it *Ghost Buster* and raked in millions in royalties!) is about Max Kearney, an advertising art director who investigates ghosts and hauntings as a hobby. This is actually a collection of nine short stories, marked by very little sense and a lot of silliness. For example, a girl is haunted by her dead father, who was a big band leader – and he brings the entire band with him to play every night… Goulart's stories tend to seem half-formed, more like notes for stories than actual stories, and they do look like they stop only when he runs out of steam. They're certainly not for everyone, but if they suit your sense of humour, they've enjoyable.
John Peel

ARSENAL ⚛⚛⚛
ENDLESS ⚛⚛⚛

CLOCKWORK'S PIRATES/GHOST BREAKER

Dutch artist Karel Thole made one of his rare excursions into US paperbacks with both covers for the Ace Double. Thole made a few appearances on the covers of early DAW Books as well. In Germany he worked mainly in the horror genre which fitted with his flair for the surreal and grotesque.

THE ARSENAL OF MIRACLES

The original art from Jack Gaughan for a 1964 Ace Double. Born in 1930, Gaughan died at an early age of 55. His first Ace SF cover was in 1962 and he went on to paint more than 30.

ADAM STRANGE
Written by Julius Schwartz
Illustrated by Murphy Anderson
Mystery in Space 53-102, DC Comics

"Quick analytical mind, flying rocket-pack, and handy ray gun..."

If there was one man I wanted to meet as a kid, it was the brilliant adventurer Adam Strange from DC's **Mystery in Space**. Created by writer Julius Schwartz and artist Murphy Anderson, his debut appearance was in DC **Showcase #17**. Archaeologist Adam Strange was used to being in tough spots, but when fleeing from savages in a hostile South American jungle, he found himself struck by the transporting Zeta Beam rocketing him to the planet Rann. Little did they know that the initial attempt of Ranagar, the first city of that alien world, to communicate with humans unexpectedly brought them Earth's first interstellar spaceman! And this guy could do everything. Of course, Strange quickly learned the language and customs from his beautiful new girlfriend Alana, and her scientist-father Sardath. Our hero soon becomes Rann's first citizen and saviour protecting the planet from all types of wild alien invasions. But the best part about this comic was the villains using bizarre weapons like huge magnifying glasses to burn their futuristic cities, or weird space vacuums to suck up their inhabitants, or even a giant pistol to blast all their precious monuments. From natural disasters to internal warfare, nothing was too complicated for Adam to solve with his quick analytical mind, flying rocket-pack, and handy ray gun. But despite Strange's deep love for Alana, he cannot remain on his adopted planet for long since the Zeta Beams effect soon wear off launching him back to Earth, where he must calculate when the next beam will strike, to be there for his next transport before it's gone.

Dave Karlen

⚛ ⚛ ⚛ ⚛

ADVENTURES OF LUTHER ARKWRIGHT
Collected edition 1997
Written and illustrated by Bryan Talbot

"Clever and multi-layered, demanding to be re-read and rewarding with previously hidden pleasures..."

I am wary of any review which describes a product as "ahead of its time", as in my experience that means it is pretentious and impenetrable. However, I can comfortably describe this comic strip as ahead of its time and give it the highest recommendation. So sophisticated is the storyline and art, even by contemporary standards, I am staggered that it is 40 years old. This graphic novel collects the first story arc, which started in in the short-lived Scottish small press SF comic **Near Myths** across the end of the 1970s and continued at another small press publisher in the UK, until it was collected by US publisher Dark Horse in the 1990s when creator Talbot rose to prominence with other projects. The adventures of an inter-dimensional freedom fighter, it tackles themes such as parallel timelines, alternative histories and the multiverse, perhaps first popularised by Michael Moorcock's fiction in the 1960s and now adopted by mainstream culture such as the recent Spiderman Multiverse animated film (which was brilliant). The story mixes Arkwright's origin with his attempts to prevent worldwide devastation by a force of "disruptors", against the background of intrigue and backstabbing in an alternative future where the Great British empire has endured but is starting to lose its grip. The story-telling is clever and multi-layered, demanding to be re-read and rewarding with previously hidden pleasures. Talbot's artwork is breath-taking in its detail and composition, not helped by Dark Horse use of a standard US comic page size when the originals where bigger, and also by having a narrow margin on the inside meaning the reader has to really bend the pages back to read all of the text. It does veer into pretension at times, in the same way that some of Alan Moore's classic comic scripts do when read decades later, but that is but a small distraction. It's been

---

THE ADVENTURES OF LUTHER ARKWRIGHT
For a Dark Horse collection of Arkwright, creator Bryan Talbot reworked a cover from Scottish comic NEAR MYTHS (see pages 14 to 15) in which Arkwright first appeared.

BEM 25
Bryan Talbot provided an early image of Luther Arkwright for this 1978 edition of a UK fanzine devoted to comic news and reviews.

ADAM STRANGE IN MYSTERY IN SPACE
Carmine Infantino pencilled and Joe Giella inked the cover for a typical Adam Strange versus outer space menace adventure.

a long time since I've read such a refreshingly original and brilliant comic.
Justin Marriott
✿ ✿ ✿ ✿

ALAS, BABYLON
Pat Frank
1959

"Other "end of the world as we know it" books have aged much better..."

One of the first books to considered what happens "the day after the bomb dropped". Colonel Mark Briggs is in Strategic Air Command Intelligence at Offutt AFB in Omaha, Nebraska. Mark's telegram to his brother Randy announces the imminent and unexpected arrival of Mark's wife and children and ends with the words 'Alas, Babylon', code for possible Armageddon. Set in Florida, it follows Randy Briggs and Mark's family to show what would happen in a small town when a US pilot inadvertently blows up a foreign port and atomic war breaks out. There's blindness from radiation burns, fallout, little to no medicine, relearning to hunt and fish to feed the family, and more radiation burns. I read this book quite a few times starting when I was a kid, but that was a long time ago. In rereading it for this article, it just hasn't held up. What really struck me was the constant casual racism that pervades the book. Several of the main characters are Black and the interaction between them and the Briggs family and between them and the town in general was a constant "Huh??" It shows how much the world has changed in the last few decades. It

was also interesting to note the naivete of the characters as they buy frozen food for freezers that will soon have no electricity and procrastinate buying needed medicines until it is too late. Other "end of the world as we know it" books such as *Lucifer's Hammer* have aged much better.
Penny Tesarek
✿ ✿

ARMAGEDDON 2419 A.D.
Philip Francis Nolan
1928

"A fun action novel..."

This is the story that pretty much defined modern science fiction (if rather simplistically) because it introduced Tony Rogers. Don't know the name? Then how about his nickname. "Buck"? Soon after, the more famous comic strip debuted, and SF became "that Buck Rogers stuff", for better or worse. The adventure starts when Buck is frozen in a cave of radioactive gases and doesn't wake up until (you guessed it!) 2419 AD. America has been invaded by Mongolian super-scientists, who've destroyed the economy, annihilated most of the population and driven the rest into hiding. They're not kidding about "Armageddon". Buck quickly gets accustomed to the future and re-introduces tactics he learned fighting in World War One to help the Americans destroy the invaders and retake their country. Oh, and he marries Wilma Deering on the way. It's a fun action novel, with one major drawback – Nolan is obsessed with making the pseudo-science he invents work. He spends page after page explaining technical details

ALAS BABYLON
1960 edition of Frank's "after the bomb dropped" novel, with an effective yet uncredited cover painting which conjured up the fiery apocalypse.

ARMAGEDDON 2419 A.D. (UK PANTHER EDITION)
1976 cover painting from Richard Clifton-Dey which was intentionally "retro" and invoked the spirit of the pulps, clearly drawing inspiration from the newspaper strip version of the character.

ARMAGEDDON 2419 A.D. (US ACE EDITION)
Ed 'Emsh' Emshwiller provided the art for this 1962 paperback compilation of Buck Rogers first two outings in Amazing Stories.

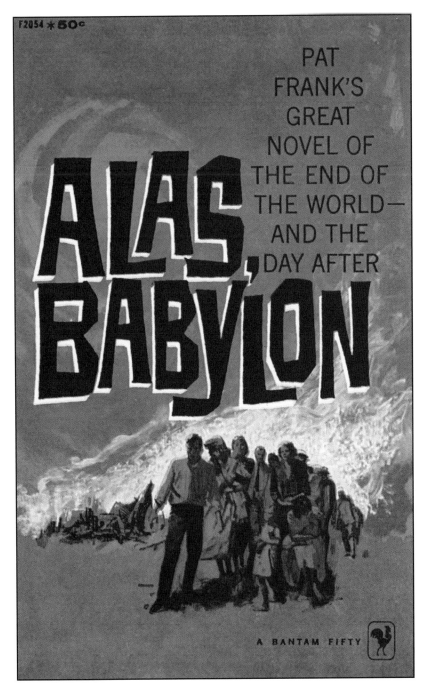

F2054 ✳ 50¢

PAT FRANK'S GREAT NOVEL OF THE END OF THE WORLD— AND THE DAY AFTER

ALAS, BABYLON

A BANTAM FIFTY

Panther Science Fiction
Armageddon 2419 AD
Philip Francis Nowlan

The Original BUCK ROGERS Novel

ace book
02935
60¢

THE ORIGINAL "BUCK ROGERS" NOVEL

ARMAGEDDON 2419 A.D.
PHILIP FRANCIS NOWLAN

Complete & Unabridged

SCOTTISH SMALL PRESS TAKES ON HEAVY METAL AND LAUNCHES THE CAREERS OF COMICS SUPERSTARS BRYAN TALBOT AND GRANT MORRISON

Five issues of this Scottish small press comic appeared sporadically over 1978 - 1980. Despite the first issue claiming to be a monthly publication, there were only three issues in 1978, and one each of the following years. Although small press, it received national distribution through David Gold & Sons, an East End based business with a focus on girlie magazines. I have vague memories of seeing it on the shelves of my local newsagents in the South West of England.

Rob King was the editor and publisher, and his debut editorial sited HEAVY METAL magazine as an inspiration and bemoaned the lack of suitable vehicles for aspiring British creators producing work in that vein. King owned the Science Fiction Bookshop in Edinburgh, which acted as an unofficial headquarters.

Bryan Talbot began his Luther Arkwright strip in issue one, and Grant Morrison wrote and drew Gideon Starbuck from issue two. It was obvious that Talbot was a massive talent, Morrison perhaps less so.

According to Bryan Talbot in a 2009 interview on the Forbidden Planet blog, "When the publisher did a moonlight flit to avoid debt, he left all the back issues in his flat. After six months the landlord dumped the lot in a skip so they're a bit rare!"

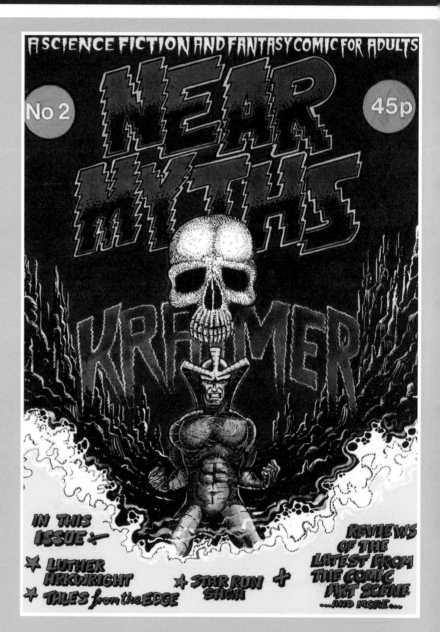

A SCIENCE FICTION AND FANTASY COMIC FOR ADULTS

No 2

45p

NEAR MYTHS

KREAMER

IN THIS ISSUE →

★ LUTHER ARKWRIGHT
★ TALES from the EDGE
★ STAR RUN SAGA

REVIEWS OF THE LATEST FROM THE COMIC ART SCENE ...AND MORE...

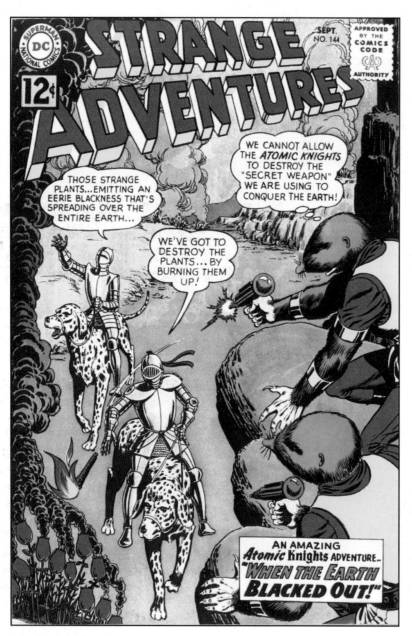

(to the point where he advises the reader to skip the next chapter at one point if the "science" bores them...). He obviously carefully worked out the plot, but it definitely gets to be too much. (Skipping the chapter works, though.) Add a star if you're fascinated to learn how "inertron" and "ultronoscopes" work.
John Peel

⚛ ⚛ ⚛

THE ATOMIC KNIGHTS
Strange Adventures 117-160
DC Comics
Written by John Broome
Art by Murphy Anderson

"They ride around on giant mutated Dalmatians..."

Back in the Sixties, DC comics had a line of SF comics that sometimes contained continuing stories – titles like **My Greatest Adventure** and **Tales of the Unexpected**. **Strange Adventures** had a run of 15 continuing stories about the Atomic Knights. They are set in 1986, following an atomic war that has destroyed most life on the planet. Gardner Grayle discovers that six old suits of armour have become impervious to radiation and can provide them protection. With five companions, he forms the Atomic Knights. And if that's not bizarre enough for you, they ride around on (and this is my favourite bit!) giant mutated Dalmatians. The Knights must face off with people who have seized power through force to exploit others. Foes include the survivors of Atlantis, who have

been blown forward through time by their own crazed experiments, and Kadey and the Blue Belts – fascists to the core. And, of course, there are all sorts of mutants, from telepathic plants to intelligent moles. Comics don't come a lot stranger – or more entertaining – than this. One of the Knights is female (and extremely cute), Marene Herald. She and Gardner are an item, but they apparently never progress beyond holding hands or stealing a quick kiss – and the stories take place over six years. Talk about your slow courtships! The stories appeared from 1960-64, though there was a revisionist attempt to "explain" how this fell into regular DC continuity Stick with the originals, now gathered into a single volume.
John Peel

⚛ ⚛ ⚛ ⚛

BARBARELLA
Jean-Claude Forest
1962

"An early forerunner to space-heroines in comics..."

Do you remember drooling over scandalous comics? Reading them under the covers by flashlight so as not to upset your moral majority parents? I was afraid they could hear all my gasps and giggles across every risqué comic page! Well in 1962, the French publication, **V-Magazine**, introduced us to a new sexy astronaut who travelled the universe righting wrongs and chasing all the handsome males from every planet she encountered. Jean-Claude Forest's **Barbarella** was an instant hit, but failed to find any favour with the French authorities, who in the later years banned all her saucy reprint book versions. As an early forerunner to space-heroines in comics, Barbarella had numerous bizarre adventures that often left her skin-tight spacesuit torn to pieces, whether fighting off wicked villains like the sadistic hunter Strikno, or using her ray gun on weird, gelatinous Jell-O pudding creatures. But one thing was for sure, Forest's elegant fine line drawings helped set the mood for the haunting and evocative romantic exploits she had with both man and machine. When the campy film adaptation starring Jane Fonda in the title role hit the silver screen in 1968, Forest tried desperately to revive the titillating feature in both France and Italy. He did not succeed until 1981, when the strip resurfaced in the pages of **L'Echo des Savanes** with Jean-Claude now just supplying bawdy

THE ATOMIC KNIGHTS IN STRANGE ADVENTURES
Issue 144 carried a rare cover appearance for the Dalmatian riding knights at a time when the covers of DC Comics non-superhero titles were dominated by dinosaurs and gorillas. Murphy Anderson art.

BARBARELLA IN THE EVERGREEN REVIEW
The famous magazine founded by renegade publisher Barney Rosset of the Grove Press became famous as a vehicle for avant-garde literature across the 50s and 60s. In 1965, it became the first American publication to feature the space heroine's strip.

scripts and Daniel Billon the spicy illustrations. Unfortunately, the liberated heroine tales did not survive long. Very sad.
Dave Karlen

✸ ✸ ✸ ✸ ✸

BONES OF THE EARTH
Michael Swanwick
2002

"Plot is muddier than water a herd of triceratops have rampaged through ..."

Palaeontologists get a chance to study dinosaurs first-hand when they're handed a time machine. Unfortunately, there's a group of Christian Fundamentalists determined to kill them so that they can't prove dinosaurs really existed. And then there's the real question – where did that time machine come from in the first place? Oh, and just to complicate things further, there are several different versions of some of the characters. And a time paradox or two. It certainly sounds like the elements for a really good adventure, and there are real hints of what it might have been. However, the characters are inconsistent, and the plot is muddier than water a herd of triceratops have rampaged through. (And, yes – that happens in the book.) It doesn't live up to its promise, and the ending doesn't actually make sense because the author's gotten tangled in his own plot convolutions. Which is a shame, really, because there's a good book in here somewhere. Maybe in another timeline?
John Peel

✸ ✸

CALLAHAN'S CROSSTIME SALOON
Spider Robinson
1974

"Silly and sentimental..."

Callahan's Crosstime Saloon has 9 chapters, with each chapter basically a stand-alone short story. The first story was originally published in **Analog** and led to Robinson winning the 1974 John W. Campbell Award for Best New Writer. Lots of fun, puns and characters, with time travelers, robots, little green men, threats to the planet averted, and an immortal who is tired of life. It's a slim book at 170 pages, but very funny, with a number of follow-up books set in the bar or involving the bar's denizens. With its short

story format, it's easy to pick up and read whenever you like. Silly and sentimental, you'll like it – I know I do!
Penny Tesarek

✸ ✸ ✸ ✸

A CANTICLE FOR LEIBOWITZ
Walter M Miller Jr
1959

"The importance of reading, truth, and knowledge..."

Unlike many "end of the world as we know it" books that begin just before the disaster hits, *A Canticle for Leibowitz* begins 6 centuries after the atomic war of the 20th century, with Brother Francis Gerard in the Utah desert near the Abbey of Leibowitz. A hero of the post-atomic decades, Isaac Leibowitz was a 'booklegger' who hid books to keep them safe from the post-war Simpleton mobs. Leibowitz was martyred by the Simpletons, who burned him and other educated people after the war. The Abbey carries on his work by copying some books to send out to the world while continuing to hide other books in kegs to keep them safe from the next wave of Simpletons. Leibowitz is currently under consideration for sainthood by the Catholic hierarchy. After a decade and half with Brother Francis, the book jumps ahead another six centuries to 3174. Civilization is doing better, with some bright and politically connected people coming to the Abbey, learning from their store of original physics texts, and generating electricity for light for the first time in 1200 years. The last section jumps another 6 centuries to 3781 (hmm, 6/6/6 centuries). Civilization now has starships – and even though much is made of the impact of radiation and the deformities it still causes among newborns, mankind has redeveloped atomic weapons and is itching to use them again. It is time for the Abbey to copy its collection, pack their bindlestiff, and seek refuge on a new planet. I've always liked how *A Canticle for Leibowitz* highlights the importance of reading, truth, and knowledge and how books must always have a safe place. It's a horror to think that we are getting to the point where we can't agree on facts or truth and that people with knowledge are treated with derision (or worse) by the simpletons of today. An excellent and thought provoking read.
Penny Tesarek

✸ ✸ ✸ ✸ ✸

CALLAHAN'S CROSSTIME SALOON
Collection of 9 short stories mainly from ANALOG
SCIENCE FICTION/SCIENCE FACT magazine. Pictured
is a 1981 reprint with a new cover painting by Vincent
Di Fate

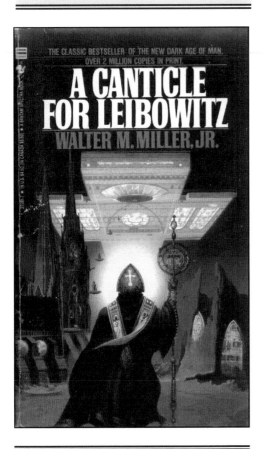

A CANTICLE FOR LEIBOWITZ
An unusual case of a cover from a British edition
(Corgi, 1979) being used on an American edition
(Bantam 1988). The artist was Peter Andrew Jones,
also known as PAJ.

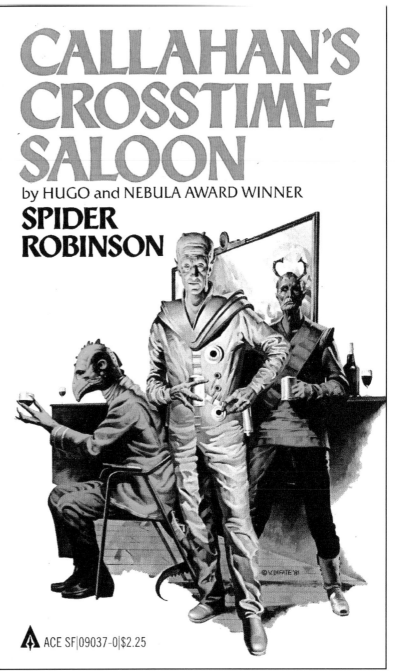

CALLAHAN'S CROSSTIME SALOON
by HUGO and NEBULA AWARD WINNER
SPIDER ROBINSON

ACE SF|09037-0|$2.25

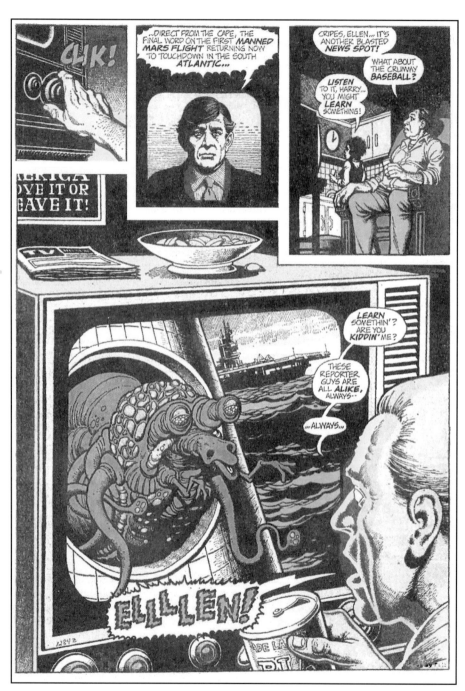

THE DAY AFTER THE DAY THE MARTIANS CAME - WORLDS UNKNOWN COMIC ADAPTATION

The criminally underrated Ralph Reese brings his quirky style of art to a Marvel Comics adaptation of the 1967 short story from Pohl which originally appeared in Harlan Ellison's *Dangerous Visions* and addressed racism. The novel reviewed is Pohl's 1988 expansion of his short story.

COLLISION COURSE

1961 Ace Double of which was paired with *The Nemesis of Terra*. Art uncredited but attributed to Ed Valigursky. The novella had appeared in a 1959 edition of AMAZING STORIES.

COLLISION COURSE
Robert Silverberg
1961

"The reader comes away with a feeling that it is all entirely plausible..."

Robert Silverberg is well known as a grandmaster of science fiction and while he has written in other genres, it is his science fiction tales that have made him a legend. With a career spanning more than 60 years, his longevity is matched only by his productivity. From 1956 to 1959, he routinely averaged five published stories a month, and he had over 80 stories published in 1958 alone. This novel, first published in 1961, takes place in the 26th century after planet Earth (Terra) has developed instantaneous transport via "transmats" making colonization of additional planets much easier. Now, during Terra's expansion into the galaxy, they've encountered an alien race which appears to be very closely matched to human evolution and level of technology and who also happens to be in the midst of expanding into the galaxy. This is essentially a first contact novel but also examines the nature of human-kind's perceptions of their own place in the universe. What appears to be a friendly alien race turns out to be rather bossy and ultimately a third, extremely powerful alien race intercedes and forces the two "child" races to negotiate an equal solution and avoid armed conflict. Unlike many "classic-era" science fiction stories, Silverberg tends to write very approachable stories rather than using obtuse and overly scientific prose. He does, however, convey an excellent competence in the nature of the science he uses, especially space travel, and the reader comes away with a feeling that it is all entirely plausible. The overall novel was fun to read, although the ending seemed a little bit like Silverberg wasn't sure where to take it. It does conclude, and the major characters are left fundamentally changed but with no commentary on what that would mean for them.
Benjamin Thomas

⚛ ⚛ ⚛ ⚛

THE DAY THE MARTIANS CAME
Frederick Pohl
1988

"I really wanted to like this novel..."

A supply rocket crashed, and the astronauts are all dying of radiation sickness. Their experiments and Scientific work have come to a screeching halt. Congress is cutting funding for the Mars program and calling it an absolute failure. Despite this, Harry keeps on drilling the surface of Mars and one day breaks through into a cavern that is eventually described as a department store. Of course, this discovery excites the people on Earth and more such exploration is encouraged. Eventually Harry drills into a cavern with what appears to be the last living Martians. Pohl's story takes on a new focus at that point. The people of Earth are energized with the idea of how this discovery affects them. For some, it brings a new sense of hope. For others, it brings a sense of doom. However, from this point in the novel the many and varied characters are looking for a way to take advantage of this discovery. The politicians use it to promote funding programs. The psychics and new age cult leaders want to promote their own scams. The script writers want to make new movies about the Martians. NASA wants to bring the Martians to Earth. As they begin to accomplish this, more and more people have to decide how this decision will affect them. Pohl's exploration of how the discovery affects earthlings is interesting and sometimes deep intellectual thinking. The influence on the discovery of these Martians to the basic psychology is explored in depth. Sadly, the novel bogs down in its intellectual exercise. The ideas presented are interesting, but the author allows himself to dwell on his character's mundane lives and their selfish response. It seems that almost every human being has their own agenda and seeks to find a way to leverage their own political, economic, and social power through this discovery. I really wanted to like this novel, but despite its efforts to present new sociological ideas, I could not enjoy it fully. Perhaps this is partially due to expecting a Martian invasion novel, but I found this novel very bland and often boring.
David "the preacher" Wilson

DEATHLOK THE DEMOLISHER
Created and illustrated by Rich Buckler
Marvel Masterworks Deathlok Volume 1

"The future is grim, the characters are grim and the hero is the grimmest of them all..."

Before there was RoboCop or the Terminator, there was Deathlok. He was a cyborg, composed of a rather unsavoury mixture of electronics and decaying flesh. He was originally a soldier named Luther Manning who was killed and his parts cryogenically frozen and then revived to become joined to the electronics side of his body. He was supposed to be a programmable killing machine, but somehow his innate humanity resurfaced and he rebelled. In an alternative future (back when the comic was produced) of 1990, he haunts the cannibal-filled streets of New York, seeking to somehow become human again and to destroy the man who created him. "Downbeat" is probably the word for this series (published in **Astonishing Tales**). The future is grim, the characters are grim, and the hero is the grimmest of them all. But, despite this, you have to empathize with Deathlok in his quest to regain everything that has been taken from him. If they had left it there, it would have been a depressing but earnest depiction of a dystopian future. But you probably know what Marvel is like – they can never leave a character with an unhappy ending. They revived him a couple of times, altering his ultimate fate over and again. And, just for good measure, they rebooted the character completely a few times. But that original run is certainly something of a classic. It's not exactly fun, but it is compelling reading.

John Peel

❁ ❁ ❁

THE DESTRUCTION OF THE TEMPLE
Barry Malzberg
1974

"What does it all mean? I have no idea..."

Quite frankly, I wouldn't have finished this book if I wasn't going to write a review. I was originally intrigued, as the cover states "winner of the John Campbell Award for the Year's Best Science Fiction Novel", only to find out that referenced the author, not this novel. Also, there were blurbs by Harlan Ellison and Robert Silverberg that I shouldn't have trusted.

In the future, the Director has gone into the city to restage the assassination of President Kennedy. In addition, throughout the novel we revisit the assassinations of Malcom X, Martin Luther King Jr., two freedom riders (Northerners who went South to help African Americans register to vote), and most oddly, George Lincoln Rockwell, leader of the American Nazi Party. There are also long passages regarding the buying of a used car to be used in the JFK assassination. What does it all mean? I have no idea. Is it supposed to be transgressive or shocking? If so, J. G. Ballard did it more effectively about 5 years earlier with "The Assassination of John Fitzgerald Kennedy Considered as a Downhill Motor Race". While there is "new wave" science fiction that I like, this would not be one of them. Give it a miss.

Tom Tesarek

DYING OF THE LIGHT
George R. R. Martin
1977

"Your enjoyment will depend on your tolerance for books that have glossaries in the back..."

Long before **Game of Thrones** or his writing for the television shows **The Twilight Zone** and **Beauty and the Beast**, George R. R. Martin was a Hugo and Nebula Award-winning author. *Dying of the Light* is his first novel, which was nominated for a Hugo, set in the 'Thousands Worlds' universe that many of

---

THE DESTRUCTION OF THE TEMPLE (FRENCH EDITION)
J'Ai Lu were a leading publisher of genre fiction in France. This is their edition of Malzberg's New Wave SF with a cover by Phillip Caza.

DYING OF THE LIGHT
1978 paperback edition of the story serialised over 4 issues of ANALOG SCIENCE FICTION/SCIENCE FACT in 1977.

DEATHLOK THE DEMOLISHER
Artist Rich Buckler ladles on the biblical imagery for the origin story of his killer cyborg in 1974.

BARRY N. MALZBERG

J'AI LU

la destruction du temple

"Wonderful, rich-tapestried. The excitement and strangeness are still there after the last sentence."
—A. E. van Vogt, author of MISSION TO THE STARS

POCKET
81130-4
$1.95

DYING OF THE LIGHT

by George R.R. Martin
Hugo Award-winning author of A SONG FOR LYA

ASTONISHING TALES

MARVEL COMICS GROUP.

25¢ 25 AUG

ASTONISHING TALES FEATURING

DEATHLOK
THE DEMOLISHER!

IS HE MAN—OR MACHINE—OR MONSTER? YOU CAN'T KNOW 'TIL YOU READ THIS SPECTACULAR FIRST ISSUE!

THE SELF-DAMNING ORIGIN OF THE WORLD'S MOST OFFBEAT SUPERHERO!

PERHAPS THE GREATEST CREATION YET! IN THE MARVEL AGE OF COMICS, PHASE TWO!

FIGHTING MAN OF MARS ORIGINAL ART

Ballantine Books were long-term US publishers of Edgar Rice Burroughs in the US. Across 1979, Ballantine reissued the Mars books with new wraparound Michael Whelan covers. In 2008, this art sold for $20k+ at auction.

ESSENTIAL ELLISON

Huge hardcover running to over 1000 pages and 80+ short stories, novellas and essays. The cover is by long-time Ellison illustrators Leo and Diane Dillon.

his short stories take place. Dirk t'Larien receives a call from his former lover Gwen Delvano. She is on the planet Worlorn, a planet that is moving through space, and while it travelled through a system with multiple suns, it was turned into a festival planet. Now as it starts to move out of the system, it had been largely deserted, except a few people who remain, like Gwen, who is an ecologist studying the interrelationship of the various flora and fauna brought to the world. Dirk finds that Gwen is "bethyn" to Jaantony and his "teyn" Janacek, from the planet High Kavalaan. Teyns are males that are bonded to each other, while bethyn is a mix of wife and property. Without giving too much away, Dirk's desire to "save" Gwen leads to a *Most Dangerous Game* style hunting of humans. Martin does an excellent job of creating the culture of High Kavalaan and explaining how that society developed concepts like teyn and bethyn as well as incorporating duelling and the hunting of people. The characters are complicated individuals, and the reader's opinion of them continually evolves throughout the novel as you discover more about their histories and cultures. I found it fascinating, but your enjoyment will depend on your tolerance for books that have glossaries in the back to provide detail on the planets, customs and alien races.
Tom Tesarek

THE ESSENTIAL ELLISON
Harlan Ellison
2001 edition

"I read this collection over many months, but I read every bit of it..."

Harlan Ellison is an absolute giant in the world of speculative fiction, as most people are aware. His short fiction is among the most often cited examples of how to "do it right" and, quite honestly, should be studied by all who endeavour to write well themselves. This massive collection includes over 80 pieces of his work including science fiction, horror, humour, main-stream fiction, and several rather pointed essays. That sounds like a lot of material, but with Ellison's output of over 1700+ stories (as of 1999), it barely scratches the surface. So how to select the proper mix of stories for such a "50 Year retrospective?" I have no idea, but the editors have done a fine job in my opinion. Included are stories from Ellison's youth, the first of which is dated 1949, as well as major classics of speculative

fiction such as "I have No Mouth and I Must Scream," "A Boy and His Dog," "'Repent, Harlequin!' Said the Ticktockman," and "The Deathbird." You'll find the classic Ellison stories in anthologies everywhere, but this volume digs deeper and allows us to take a sort of journey along his career (at least up until 2001 when this was published). We are also exposed to several essays which shed an honest light on Ellison's rather notorious 'mean-spiritedness.' It's refreshing to read his side of the story and while it's evident that he is not a person to be bullied, his masterful ability with the written word, even in a letter to a publisher, is fascinating. I read this collection over many months, but I read every bit of it. I've come away with a deep appreciation for Ellison's work as well as his approach to life. If I had to pick one piece within this collection that was most inspiring, it would not be a story at all but rather his "Introduction to 'Tired Old Man'", written in 1975. It describes what Ellison, himself, considers among his favourites of his own work and describes how it came to be written, based on an apparent supernatural experience of the author's. A truly great collection. Highly recommended.
Benjamin Thomas

A FIGHTING MAN OF MARS
Edgar Rice Burroughs
1930

"One thing you can guarantee from any ERB novel is a thundering good adventure tale..."

You can always tell when you're reading any book by Edgar Rice Burroughs, because his heroes are skilled warriors, his heroines beautiful (and generally princesses, at the very least) and the coincidences in the stories are staggering. If the party comes across a prisoner, it's usually either (a) one of the party's long-lost loves; (b) one of the party's long-lost parents; or, occasionally (c) both. And in his Mars series, they also inevitably run into a mad scientist who has invented a new kind of death ray or killing machine. And – you know what? You just don't care. Because one thing you can guarantee from any ERB novel is a thundering good adventure tale. He's always exciting and you just put everything else aside. This book is a perfect example of his stereotype – Hadron of Hastor is the Fighting Man, and he's off to rescue the woman he loves, who has (of course) been kidnapped by the evil warlord

RICHARD CLIFTON·DEY

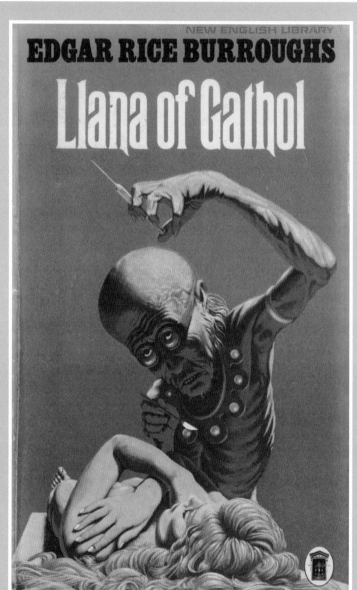

NEW ENGLISH LIBRARY
EDGAR RICE BURROUGHS
Llana of Gathol

CULT UK PUBLISHER NEW ENGLISH LIBRARY PACKAGED THEIR 60S AND 70S EDITIONS OF EDGAR RICE BURROUGHS PAPERBACKS WITH COVERS THAT WERE VIBRANT, SEXY AND ALLURING

New English Library and its predecessor Four Square, issued a steady stream of Edgar Rice Burroughs across the 1960s and into the 70s, specifically the Tarzan, Mars and Venus books. They are a collector's dream in that they were often in a uniform design, sometimes numbered, and always carried gorgeous cover art.

Although I imagine some would argue that Josh Kirby's series of images for the ERB Mars books were the finest of these, but for me it is clearly Richard Clifton Dey, known as Dick by his colleagues. Clifton-Dey would become famous for his series of western covers featuring anti-hero Edge, but started his career at New English Library on a variety of genres, showing a flair for historical adventure and science fiction.

His Burroughs covers often used coloured backgrounds to suggest an other-worldliness, reds, purples and greens representing the atmospheres on far-flung worlds. All of which contrasted with the realism of his figure work, and his command of anatomy resulted in is alien creations carrying a heft. The original art for *Wizard of Venus*, with its green background and convincing alien-horse being a prime example.

The first printings of the books with Clifton-Dey art carried the distinctive white font for the title - see *Llana of Gathol*. Reprints introduced a number for the series inside a circle and a type-font for the author name and book title.

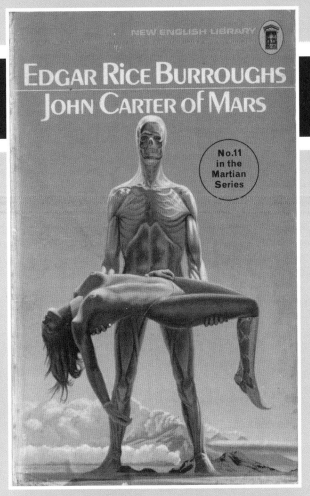

NEW ENGLISH LIBRARY

EDGAR RICE BURROUGHS
JOHN CARTER OF MARS

No. 11 in the Martian Series

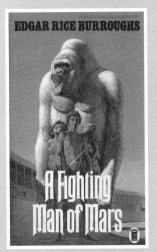

EDGAR RICE BURROUGHS

A Fighting Man of Mars

EDGAR RICE BURROUGHS

SWORDS OF MARS

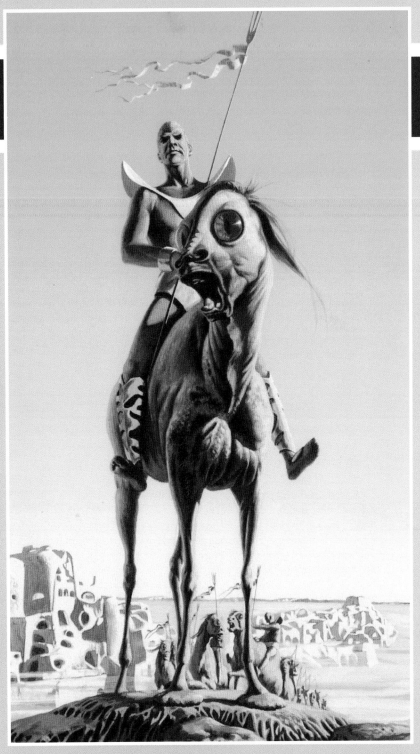

wanting to conquer Mars. Mad scientist? Check. Illogical coincidences? Check. Missing loves/relatives? Double check. But fun? Constantly. So buckle on your swashes, and head along for a blooming good romp.

John Peel

✺ ✺ ✺

FLASH GORDON 1: THE LION MEN OF MONGO
Con Steffanson (Ron Goulart)
1977

"Old-fashioned sword and sandal adventure story..."

The grand ol' era of Flash Gordon comic strips was, alas, before my time. Same goes for the Saturday matinee serials. But he remains such an iconic character that I've long wanted to learn more about him and all the supporting characters, as well as the creator, Alex Raymond. This novel seemed like a good place to start, being the first of a dozen or so books "inspired" by the original comic strip. Indeed, while Alex Raymond's name is credited on the cover, this was actually adapted by "Con Steffanson" a pseudonym used by Ron Goulart, a noted American popular cultural historian and prolific novelist in his own right. This first novel sets it all up nicely. Flash Gordon, Dale Arden, and Dr. Zarkov are on a survey mission over the planet Mongo when they are forced to crash land. All three are separated from one another from the beginning and have separate adventures on their way to meeting up near the end of the book. We get a good introduction to what life is like on Mongo, both in terms of the strange creatures as well as the current political situation. We get to meet Ming in all his merciless glory as he attempts to bring the rest of Mongo under his diabolical control. Flash has a nice set of mini adventures with Tun, a member of the Lion Men. Zarkov meets and works with a group of scientists and, unfortunately, Dale spends most of her time as Ming's captive and potential concubine. We are also introduced to other soon-to-be major players such as Ming's daughter Aura and Prince Barin, although the latter is mostly by reputation until an actual cameo appearance at the very end. I enjoyed reading this one. It's an easy-going style as I expected, with short chapters usually ending with a cliff-hanger. The POV jumps around a lot among the three major characters with an occasional viewpoint from others, such as Ming. It's an old-fashioned

sword and sandal adventure story, just what I was hoping for as an introduction to the Flash Gordon universe.

Benjamin Thomas

✺ ✺ ✺ ✺

FLASH GORDON #3: THE SPACE CIRCUS
Con Steffanson (Ron Goulart)
1980

"He needs to be treated seriously and not as some kind of a joke..."

Flash Gordon is one of the more famous characters in science fiction literature. Created and drawn by Alex Raymond, he started life as a daily comic strip before making his mark in the old movie serials. In the Seventies, Avon Books revived the character in a series of six novels that adapted the old strips. In this adventure, Flash is kidnapped by slavers and sold to... well, obviously, a space circus. Flash being Flash, he manages to lead a breakout of slaves into the jungles of the planet Mesmo. It's all hokey fun, of course, filled with plenty of action and staggering coincidences, as many of these stories from the Thirties and Forties tended to be. The idea of the series, though, would seem to have been that Ron Goulart (under one of his many pen-names) was to have updated the books and made them more contemporary. The problem there, though, is that Goulart has a style of his own which aged faster than Alex Raymond's. He liked to write light-hearted parodies, infused with plenty of silliness. And that doesn't sit very well with **Flash Gordon**. He needs to be treated seriously and not as some kind of a joke. Try the original strips – they're dated, but enjoyable – and give these books a miss.

John Peel

✺

FLESHPOTS OF SANSATO
William F Temple
1970 (abridged version)

"Layers and symbolism to the story that were lost to me ..."

Described as "space-opera", possibly because of the central story of a secret agent pursuing a renegade scientist and possibly because people like simple-minded labels. Temple's final novel is one that I wanted to enjoy but ultimately found

FLASH GORDON: THE SPACE CIRCUS

1974 edition of the third in a series of six novels based on the Alex Raymond comic strips. George Wilson painted new covers for the paperbacks.

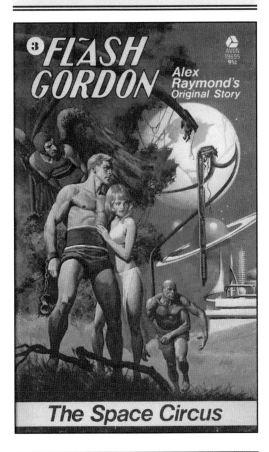

THE FLESHPOTS OF SANSATO

1970 paperback edition of Temple's final novel carried a suitably gaudy painting by Bruce Pennington. Pennington was prolific across the 70s and his style has proved influential but difficult to replicate.

a struggle. A British super-fan and ex-house-mate of Arthur C Clarke, turned author, Temple apparently quit writing due to the editing employed by the editors of the 1970 paperback edition issued by UK publisher New English Library. Although there were no other English language editions derived from the 1968 hardback, so I imagine that it was not entirely the fault of the editors that the book is a confusing and lacklustre read. Especially for one set on an interplanetary equivalent of Las Vegas with all of its many excesses and potential for satire, which cover artist Bruce Pennington was requested to focus on for his purple-drenched illustration. Temple was more effective in the short story form, and there are several excellent sequences in this novel which could have worked very well on that basis, such as the opening sequence where the manipulative head of the spy agency reflects on his life, or the description of the seven rooms of a brothel and the sexual mastery of the prostitute that works there. I sense there were layers and symbolism to the story that were lost to me, so perhaps there are greater pleasures to be derived from the fleshpots than I could manage.

Justin Marriott

✵ ✵

FOOTPRINTS OF THUNDER
James F. David
1995
"Terrific read that holds attention from beginning..."
Combines elements of science fiction, the adventure novel and the end of the world thriller, in an entertaining tale of

---

THE THING FROM ANOTHER WORLD (UK CHERRY TREE EDITION)
Considered one of the rarest SF paperbacks of all time, this 1952 UK edition used the film title on its cover, but kept the original title of 'Who Goes There?' inside.

WHO GOES THERE?
1951 US hardcover which formed the basis of the UK 1952 edition.

FROZEN HELL
2019 edition restoring Campbell's original manuscript.

---

rampaging dinosaurs and time travel. When a freak phenomenon dissolves the boundaries between yesterday and today, the world is transformed into a patchwork mixture of the present and the past. Cities like Atlanta have disappeared to be replaced by forest and ancient tundra landscapes, while dinosaurs stalk the streets of New York and swim in the oceans. The world is thrown into chaos, as scientists desperately try to work out what happened and reverse it before governments destroy what is left. It is an intriguing and clever concept and David makes good use of it, as he takes his large cast of mainly American characters through the unfolding disaster. David is very good at showing, rather than telling, and we mainly see the effects of the 'time quilting' through the eyes of ordinary citizens as they come to grips with the weirdness around them. There are brief scenes in which scientists try to explain to the President what has happened, but it is the individual experiences that drive the story. David wisely does not spend too much effort trying to explain how it happened, but instead gives the reader great, and often moving, vignettes of encounters with dinosaurs and the efforts of people to re-unite with their loved ones. The book moves along at a brisk pace and is a terrific read that holds attention from beginning to end. Great fun.

Jeff Popple

✵ ✵ ✵ ✵

FROZEN HELL
Joseph W. Campbell
2019 version
"Enjoyed how the characters talked over and around each other...reminded me of the...Howard Hawks film!"

In 1938, a longish short story, "Who Goes There?", appeared in the pages of **Astounding Magazine**. The story was credited to Don A. Stuart, a pseudonym for John W. Campbell. This was to be one of the last pieces of fiction Campbell wrote, as much of the rest of his life would be spent as Chief Editor of that same magazine. Behind the scenes, the story had undergone rejections and rewrites before becoming the trimmed product that the public saw. The original draft was filed away and forgotten until 2019. As most of us know, this story became one of the top SF tales of all time and has been filmed three times under the tile *The Thing* (*The Thing from Another Planet* was the full name of the first film version). Short Version: An alien craft and lifeform are discovered under the ice in Antarctica and does its best to escape to more populated areas with the help of its superpower – the ability to mimic any person or creature with which it can make blood contact! The part trimmed for publication was the beginning, where a scouting team from an Antarctic research station finds an object under the ice in an area many miles south of their main camp. This portion includes some character development, which was verboten in the Golden Age of SF. Most interesting is the painting of main character MacReady as a very jocular and optimistic fellow. This is contraindicative of Wold Newtonian theories that he was actually a young Clark Savage, Jr. acting under a non de plume! From here, the action proceeds furiously. With some very quick exposition (too quick?), the scientists discover the methods of the alien creature(s) and try various methods to root out any imposters. I really enjoyed how the characters talked over and around each other; it reminded me of the quick patter of the Howard Hawks film! Plus, there is one other power the alien possesses, that did not make it into the film versions, and it's a creepy doozy that I'll let you discover on your own!!

Scott Ranalli

⚛ ⚛ ⚛ ⚛

GLADIATOR-AT-LAW
Fredrik Pohl and C. M. Kornbluth
1955

"A tremendous amount going on..."

In the future, people either live in a GML home, a marvel of technology, or in one of the numerous slums like Belly Rave. Charles Mundin is a lawyer who is just barely getting by when he gets Norma and Don Lavin, the L in GML homes, as clients. Their father, who created the homes, wanted them to be available to everyone, but he was pushed out by his business partners, who lease them to corporations. The corporations provide them to their employees, giving the corporations tremendous power over their workers. If you lose your job, you lose your house, and you are on your way to the dangerous slums. The Lavins' now live in Belly Rave and are trying to regain control of GML. Mundin agrees to help them against the extremely powerful people who are happy with the status quo. Norvell Bligh was a designer of the gladiatorial games that are used as an outlet for people's violent urges, especially for those living in the slums. He loses his job and his house and is forced to move to Belly Rave with his wife and

step-daughter, who lived there before they were married. The scenes in Belly Rave are fascinating. When they arrive, they move into one of the many vacant, decaying houses. The spoiled daughter is told by the mother to shape up or be sold. Norvel is shocked, and his wife explains "It's easy, you can always find a Fagin or a madam for a kid...when I was thirteen, I brought fifty dollars." To avoid this fate, kids join youth gangs like the Wabbits, who carry broken bottles and are ready to use them. Bligh ends up working with Mundin on the Lavins' case. *Gladiator-at-Law* is an odd mix of topics and is difficult to summarize, as there is a tremendous amount going on in this relatively short book. There are long sections on corporate governance and legal manoeuvres that may make some readers' eyes glaze over, and the gladiatorial aspects are surprisingly minor, given the title of the book. However, I found it fascinating and the book as a whole is well worth a quick read.

Tom Tesarek

⚛ ⚛ ⚛ ⚛

THE GLORY THAT WAS
L. Sprague de Camp
1952

"Two modern men living with the discomforts inherent in a pre-technological civilization..."

In the 27th Century there's an Emperor of the World, but he's more a figurehead than a political leader. Still, he has enough pull to arrange to have Greece surrounded by an impenetrable force field. When people of Greek descent begin to vanish, two-fisted journalist Knut Bulnes decides to investigate. With him is portly classical scholar Wiyem Flin, whose wife is among the missing. The two figure out a way to bypass the force field in Bulnes' yacht, but the boat is then rammed and sunk by what appears to be an ancient Greek trireme. Getting ashore, the two men find themselves in what is apparently Greece in the time of Perikles, just before the Peloponesian War breaks out. But have they gone back in time, or is it all an elaborate hoax? Much of the story depends on Bulnes and Flin figuring out a way to answer this question. de Camp takes the bizarre premise and moves the story along logically within that framework, building up a nice level of suspense and inserting a couple of well-described action scenes. He also has a lot of fun dealing with two modern people living with the discomforts

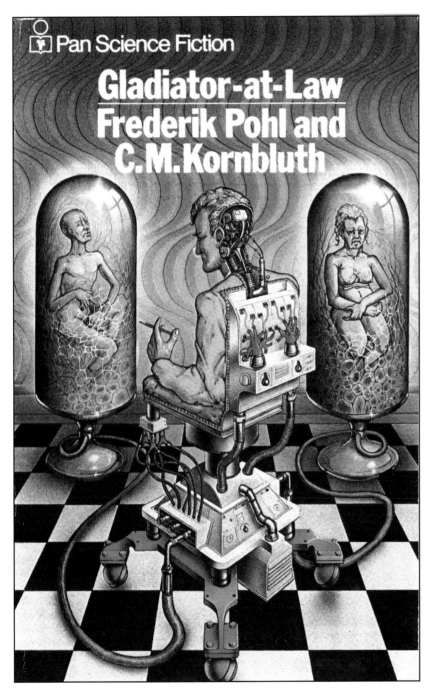

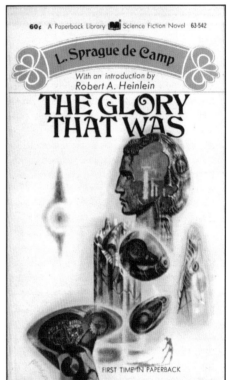

GLADIATOR-AT-LAW
Patrick Woodroffe provided a typically bizarre and ornate illustration for this 1974 UK edition from Pan Books. Woodroffe was successful in the UK but never made the journey into US paperbacks. A recommended collection is *Mythopoeikon*.

THE GLORY THAT WAS
The first paperback edition of Sprague de Camp's novel which was expanded from his novella which appeared in a 1952 issue of STARTLING STORIES. Cover by Richard Powers.

THE HIGH CRUSADE
1964 US paperback edition of the serial that appeared in ASTOUNDING in 1960. Cover art by Richard Powers.

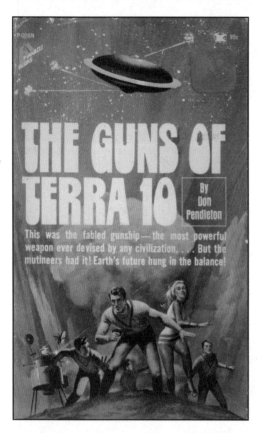

THE GUNS OF TERRA 10
Don Pendleton is now best remembered as the creator of the vigilante genre with his The Executioner series. Before that success, Pendleton turned his hand to any genre including softcore sleaze and action-SF, such as this 1970 title.

inherent in a pre-technological civilization. The humour is never mean-spirited--it simply plays off the foibles of human nature. And that humour never interferes with the novel's main task of telling an adventure story.

Tim Deforest

⚛ ⚛ ⚛ ⚛

THE GODDESS OF GANYMEDE
Michael D. Resnick
1968

"Follows the old formula (too) strictly beat by beat..."

Soldier-of-fortune and astronaut Adam Thane is sent on a secret space mission to Jupiter. He crash-lands on the moon of Ganymede, where the low gravity gives him superhuman strength. Captured by the winged Kroths who look like demons but are basically decent and good swordsmen, Thane learns the language and joins his hosts as a warrior. They get forced into a war by the human-like, evil and immortal Malthor whose leader Tarafolga wants to marry princess Delisse against her will. But Adam Thane has sworn to rescue the beautiful girl. Decades before Mike Resnick became a Hugo award winning writer, he began his career with Edgar Rice Burroughs pastiches. *The Goddess of Ganymede* is not badly written for a first published novel, and it frankly acknowledges its roots in the dedication. But a really good pastiche needs at least some memorable variation of the theme. This is lacking. The problem is not that the plot strictly follows the old formula beat by beat. More disappointing is the setting, which offers little that is interesting or colourful. Frankly Moorcock, Bulmer and Carter did this kind of book better. But you have to applaud the effort of the editorial of Paperback Library. Aside a wonderful cover by artist Jeff Jones there are also six full-page B&W illustrations by Neal MacDonald. Many writers first published novel got a much, much poorer showcase for their efforts.

Andreas Decker

⚛ ⚛

THE GUNS OF TERRA 10
Don Pendleton
1970

"Action enlivens this tale, but there's also some nice philosophic brooding..."

Don Pendleton is best known as the creator of the ultra-violent books about **The Executioner**, so I'll be honest upfront – I really wasn't expecting much from a science fiction novel of his. To my amazement, I ended up really enjoying this very different story. Hundreds of years in the future, humanity has been subjected to genetic manipulation, creating variations who are suited to their specific tasks, such as our hero, Gunner Zachary Whaleman, who has been bred to command the awesome gunship Terra 10, the last line of defence for the Earth. As with everything, though, there are failures in this DNA assignment, ending up with Reevers – reversions to the old-style humans. Considered inferior, they are restricted to Earth, and forced to work only as farmers, confined under strict regulations. They hit upon a plan to kidnap the Gunner and gain control of Terra 10. With his help, they plan to hold Earth hostage with the guns of the title to gain their freedom. Of course, things go very wrong when the first aliens discovered by humanity send a fleet to the Earth to destroy the human race... Plenty of action enlivens this tale, but there's also some nice philosophic brooding. And – rather amusingly – a hero who has a definite Oedipus complex, who keeps thinking about his mother's boobs...

John Peel

⚛ ⚛ ⚛ ⚛

THE HIGH CRUSADE
Poul Anderson
1960

"Pure fun from start to finish..."

Sir Roger is my hero. I want to be just like him when I grow up. Heck, when an alien spaceship lands in medieval England, expecting the primitive savages who live there to panic at the first laser blast, Sir Roger rallies his men and charges the spaceship. Longbow shafts pincushion the guy with the laser pistol and the armoured knights turn the battle into a hand-to-hand affair. Advanced aliens with lasers and atomic weapons haven't the faintest idea how to do hand-to-hand combat. All but one of them die and Sir Roger has himself a spaceship. He doesn't know how to fly the darn thing, but his prisoner does. Sir Roger's plan? Use the huge ship to transport not just his military force, but his entire town (men, women, children and livestock) to the Continent to kick some French butt, then maybe liberate the Holy Land afterwards. When the alien tricks him by locking in the auto-pilot to take them all to another planet, Sir Roger still doesn't lose his cool. Instead, he rams the ship into an alien base and turns yet another battle into a hand-to-hand affair. But the displaced humans are now stuck on another world, with the navigational records that would allow them to find Earth again destroyed. From there, the doughty knight improvises wildly, convincing several sets of aliens that his small army is stronger and better equipped than it really is. Through guile, diplomacy, outright lies and force of will, he wins another battle, gains some allies and begins to overthrow a huge empire, setting up an intergalactic feudal system in its place. *The High Crusade* is pure fun from start to finish.

Tim Deforest

� ✺ ✺ ✺ ✺

INFERNO
Larry Niven and Jerry Pournelle
1976

"Explanations that get more and more outlandish..."

Allen Carpentier, a writer of hard science fiction, manages to accidently kill himself while drunkenly trying to impress some fans at an SF convention. He regains consciousness, but cannot see, hear or feel anything. Trapped with his thoughts, over time he starts to go mad, finally screaming "for the love of God, get me out of here!" At that point he regains his body, and is confronted by Benito, who informs him that he is in Hell, which Carpentier doesn't believe. It turns out that Dante's description of Hell is correct, and Benito, acting as Virgil to Carpentier's Dante, leads him through the various circles of Hell, as the only way to escape is by descending to the bottom. In each circle they meet damned souls that fit that circle's criteria. My education did not include studying Dante's *Inferno*, so I am sure that I missed many of the references, but I still enjoyed the novel. It was fun figuring out who Niven and Pournelle were referencing, and it was no surprise that the Circle of Heretics included L. Ron Hubbard, but I was surprised at how negative they were towards Kurt Vonnegut, who was also there.

At one point, Carpentier states "Why him. A science fiction writer who lied about writing science fiction because he made more money that way". While I shouldn't attribute the statements of a character to the authors, that one does sound like sour grapes. I think my favourite aspect of the novel is that Carpentier doesn't believe that he is in Hell and so he comes up with science fiction explanations that get more and more outlandish for all of the supernatural events that he encounters. While I don't think this is Niven and Pournelle's best book, it is an enjoyable read.

Tom Tesarek

✺ ✺ ✺

THE LATHE OF HEAVEN
Ursula K. Le Guin
1971

"Highly readable, thoughtful fantasy..."

When I was a teenager, quality SF on television was a rarity. However, one exception was the Public Television adaptation of *The Lathe of Heaven*, which focused on ideas instead of special effects. While I really enjoyed it, for some reason I never got around to reading the book. This all-review issue gives me a chance to rectify this oversight. George Orr has been caught using other people's pharmacy cards to get drugs to stop him from dreaming. As punishment, he is sent to Dr. William Haber, a psychiatrist who specializes in dreams. George believes that he sometimes has "effective dreams" that

---

INFERNO - SPANISH EDITION
1990 edition in Spanish language with a cover by Alberto Sole who started his career as a comic artist in westerns.

INFERNO - UK EDITION
Peter Andrew Jones illustration on a 1977 UK edition.

THE LATHE OF HEAVEN
1974 Panther UK edition with a cover painting by Colin Hay. It is typical of Hay's work in that belongs in the 'hardware' genre originated by Chris Foss with detailed images of future tech and architecture.

CIENCIA FICCIÓN

INFERNO

Un viaje alucinante a los abismos
de un infierno neodantesco por los autores de
La paja en el ojo de Dios y **El martillo de Lucifer**

Larry Niven & Jerry Pournelle
INFERNO

Panther Science Fiction

Hugo and Nebula Award-winning author

URSULA K. LeGUIN
The Lathe of Heaven

0 586 03841 8

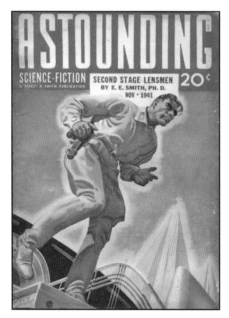

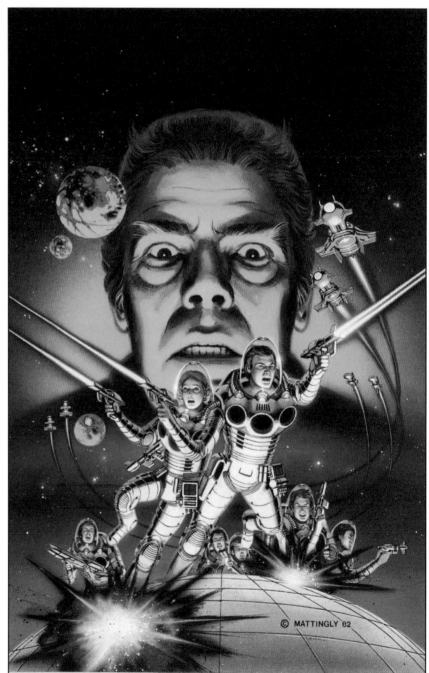

change reality. Slowly Dr. Haber realizes that George is correct and starts to shape his dreams using a dream Augmenter. In general, Haber starts small, improving the weather, and improving his professional standing. However, he then starts to attempt to radically improve the world. Let's end overpopulation-plague wipes out the majority of people. Let's end all wars/conflicts between people-cue an alien attack that unifies Earth. Let's end racial strife-now everyone is grey. Nothing works out quite the way as Haber hopes, as the methods that George's dreams deal with the problems just create new problems. I really enjoyed that this book had no villains. Haber is operating with the best of intentions, but as the saying goes, the road to hell is paved with good intentions. Science Fiction can be thought-provoking, and this novel is an excellent example.

Tom Tesarek

❀ ❀ ❀ ❀

THE LENSMAN SERIES
E. E. (Doc) Smith
1934-48

"You might read these books and think that there are a bunch of clichés – but you'd be wrong..."

When I was a kid, my Mom had a drawer of paperbacks in the buffet in the kitchen. In amongst the Tarzan, Doc Savage, Lin Carter and Edgar Cayce books was the entire six volume Lensman series. I read all of the books in that drawer many

---

LONE STAR PLANET IN FANTASTIC UNIVERSE, MARCH 1957
Lone Star Planet started a 63 page novella which appeared behind a Virgil Finlay cover. It was reprinted as A Planet for Texans as half of an Ace Double in 1958. Then returned to its original title for a 1979 edition.

LENSMEN IN ASTOUNDING STORIES, NOVEMBER 1941
The first of four parts of the third published Lensmen was in this classic mag with a Hubert Rogers cover.

LENSMEN ORIGINAL ART
David Mattingly provided retro-style covers for Berkley Books reissues of the Lensmen series across 1982.

---

times, they are seared in my brain. The series begins in Triplanetary, out in space with the conflict between two alien species (the good Arisians and the evil Eddorians). Help is needed – so the Arisians begin influencing various species' evolution. As these species learn spaceflight, they form the Galactic Patrol. To help the Galactic Patrol in their efforts to maintain law and order while reducing the drug trade among the thousands of inhabited planets, Arisia gave the Patrol the Lens. As each Lensman graduates from the academy, he meets with Mentor of Arisia for mental training and to be fitted with his Lens, which will work only for him and kill any other entity who tries to wear it. With the Lens, the Lensman can understand any language, becomes telepathic, and can use his Lens to beam thoughts across the two Galaxies instantaneously. The Lensman series follows Earth's Kinnison family as the Arisians help each generation fight the Eddorians while finding the best gal to marry and have kids. By the time we get to Children of the Lens, Kim Kinnison (now a Second Stage Lensman) and his wife Clarissa (the Red Lensman) have one son and four daughters. The planned 7th book was not written, but Doc Smith did say that anyone who has read the books knows what will happen next. You might read these books and think that there are a bunch of clichés – but you'd be wrong. Doc Smith was first on the scene – those are original ideas and scenarios! At times, the books do read like they are approaching 100 years old. There isn't the casual racism of Tarzan, but there are some pretty old science ideas (no, there isn't an ether in space for the spaceships to fly through). Unlike 700-page behemoths written 80 years later, these are quick reads (coming in at 200 pages each) and the space opera keeps the story hopping. Clear Ether!

Penny Tesarek

❀ ❀ ❀

LONE STAR PLANET
H. Beam Piper
1957

"Works as a science-fiction adventure story and as a funny political/cultural parody..."

On the planet New Texas, controlling a herd of gigantic cattle requires armoured vehicles, making each rancher the owner of a private army. There is a central government, but it can't do much. If, for instance, a politician starts pushing for an income tax or gun control, someone will simply kill him. The assassin is then tried at the Court of Political Justice. If he can make an effective defence that the killing was justified because the politician was overstepping his authority, he is acquitted. This is the situation into which Stephen Silk, ambassador from Earth is thrust. He is tasked with bringing New Texas into the Earth-run Solar League. But the previous ambassador had been killed and Silk realizes he is being set up for assassination as well. His death will then be used as an excuse for New Texas to simply be annexed. In fact, he's pretty sure members of his own staff have orders to kill him. Silk must learn how to play New Texas' unique game of deadly politics. If he can pull this off, he might just stay alive as well as actually negotiate a treaty. *Lone Star Planet* works as a science-fiction adventure story and as a funny political/cultural parody that never crosses a line into being mean-spirited.

Roy Nugen

�✿✿✿✿

LUCIFER'S HAMMER AND FOOTFALL
Larry Niven and Jerry Pournelle
1977 & 1985

"The authors had a ton of fun writing the second version..."

One may ask, aren't each of the books in this fine Marriot publication supposed to be reviewed separately? Why, oh why, is this a review of 2 different books?? Answer: It isn't. Basically, these are the same stories and work best with a single review. Apparently, the authors pitched the idea of the space alien Fithp coming to Earth on a one-way trip, finding us humans on their planet, and them terraforming (ooops, fithpforming) the Earth's climate by tossing asteroids into the oceans to make the world more to their liking. The publisher said "Hey, great idea, but can you lose the aliens and just make it an asteroid?" – so they did. *Lucifer's Hammer* is the asteroid/no aliens version of the story issued in 1977 and nominated for a Hugo award. Several years later, Larry & Jerry wrote the aliens version, which was nominated for a Hugo and a Locus. Both books are a lot of fun to read with characters and subplot galore. Each book has a USA politician playing a big role in determining what to do about the problem and how to survive once the asteroid(s) hit, the gruff but loveable guitar playing biker who knows the political folks and does his best to help out (although his best is rather lacking

at times), the Russian cosmonauts working with the USA in space (shades of Apollo/Soyez) , and the plucky gals who help keep humanity alive / fight the aliens. You can tell that the authors had a ton of fun writing the second version; one subplot is a gaggle of science fiction writers trying to understand and counteract the aliens (bonus points for every author you can identify). I reread and enjoyed both books multiple times back in the '90's and '00's – especially the minutia of spaceflight, the military, space-based weapons (including one that Jerry invented while working at Boeing), and what would happen if a big asteroid hit the planet. However, I must admit that the changes in the world in the last 20 years have made many of the details of the space interaction inexplicable for anyone who wasn't around during the 1970's and 1980's and reduced the number of stars accordingly. That said, they are still fun books and highly recommended!

Penny Tesarek

LUCIFER'S HAMMER ✿✿✿
FOOTFALL ✿✿✿✿

LUCKY STARR AND THE MOONS OF JUPITER
Paul French (Isaac Asimov)
1957

"Another aspect of Asimov's "3 Laws of Robotics" in action..."

The Lucky Starr books were written by Isaac Asimov under the pseudonym of "Paul French", and therein lies a tale. In 1951 Asimov met with his agent, Frederik Pohl, and Walter I. Bradbury, then the science fiction editor at Doubleday. They proposed that Asimov write a juvenile science fiction novel that would serve as the basis for a television series. Reportedly, Asimov feared that the novel would be adapted into what he called the "uniformly awful" programming he saw flooding the television airwaves, so he decided to publish it under the pseudonym "Paul French". The TV show never materialized but Asimov would go on to write six Lucky Starr novels. This is the fifth book in the series and finds David "Lucky" Starr and his sidekick, John "Bigman" Jones (all 5'2" of him) on a mission to the moons of Jupiter to try and determine how a top-secret experimental technology is being sabotaged...and stop that from happening. Even though couched in a young adult science fiction package Asimov, as usual, provides a compelling

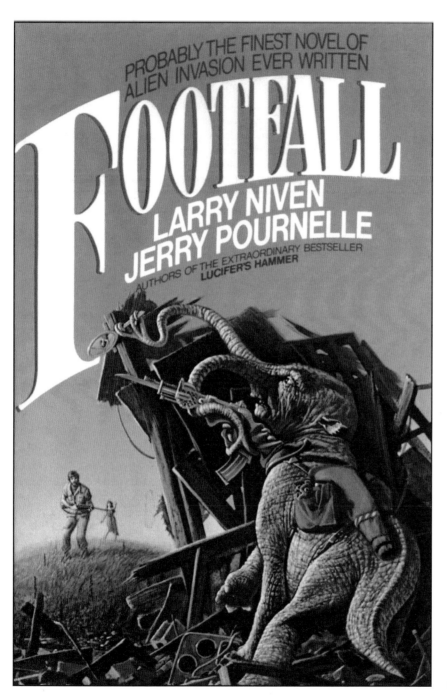

PROBABLY THE FINEST NOVEL OF ALIEN INVASION EVER WRITTEN

FOOTFALL

LARRY NIVEN
JERRY POURNELLE

AUTHORS OF THE EXTRAORDINARY BESTSELLER
LUCIFER'S HAMMER

THE MOONS OF JUPITER
In the early 1970s, prolific UK publisher of SF New English Library, issued The Lucky Starr books under Asimov's name, rather than the pseudonym of Paul French, and with no suggestion they had been written for the juvenile market. Bruce Pennington cover.

FOOTFALL
A beautiful wraparound cover by Michael Whelan graced this Del Rey/Ballantine edition from 1985. Covers for other editions were uniformly dull by comparison.

adventure injected with a fair amount of astronomy and physics education. At its core, this is a detective story, but it's also more than that. Here, David Starr, as a Councilman (of the distinguished "Council of Science") must ingratiate himself with a group of suspicious remote space station crew members, discover the identity of the saboteur among them, trick a robot, and keep his sidekick under control. No easy task. It was nice to see another aspect of Asimov's "3 Laws of Robotics" in action. This has always been a compelling idea for me, especially when odd situations require unique interpretations of the laws by the robot in question. As is often the case with vintage science fiction, the novel is quite dated. To see these advanced space-faring people using punch cards, tape reels, and printers to decipher computer codes is fun for those of us who have lived through the stone age of computer technology but reading it now...well readers will need to forgive Mr. Asimov for not foreseeing the rapidity of such change to come. All in all, this was a quick fun read just as the other Lucky Starr books have been.

Benjamin Thomas

�֎ ✷ ✷ ✷

MAGNUS, ROBOT FIGHTER 4000 A.D.
Gold Key Comics, 1963 - 1977
Russ Manning

"Space pirates, aliens, wicked robots..."

Way before Skynet became "self-aware", and Sarah Conner fought the Terminator, we had another cyborg busting champion. With his first appearance in **Magnus, Robot Fighter 4000 A.D.** #1 in 1963, writer and artist Russ Manning created a new **Tarzan** inspired character for the distant future. After working on Edgar Rice Burroughs Jungle Lord for Gold Key and the newspaper syndicate, Manning got a chance to do his own series at Western Publishing and decided to update the

MAGNUS ROBOT FIGHTER - ORIGINAL ART FOR ISSUE ONE
George Wilson's cover for the 1963 Gold Key comic. Russ Manning, creator and key artist for the character provided a sketch, which Wilson finished.

Ape Man mythos. But instead of being raised by primates, Magnus was reared by a benevolent robot called 1A who foresaw a very grim future in mankind's growing dependence on the metal-men. Trained by 1A, Magnus is a warrior sworn to protect humans from rogue machines and the humans who used them for their own evil purposes. Instructed in an advanced martial art, our gladiator can break steel with his bare hands and is equipped with a telepathic device in his skull to "hear" all robot-to-robot communications. Magnus is soon the guardian of the sprawling city of North Am battling space pirates, aliens, wicked robots and other various threats. With the help of his lovely girlfriend, Leeja Clane, her senator father, Victor Clane, and a boy's club known as "The Outsiders," Magnus has many exciting adventures done in Manning's sleek streamline style for the first twenty-one issues, before Russ left the feature. Paul Norris was chosen to take over the artwork for most of the remaining tales, along with lots of reprints to round out the series before it ended with issue #46 in January of 1977. The First Law: A ROBOT SHALL NOT HARM A HUMAN...

Dave Karlen

✷ ✷ ✷ ✷

THE MAN WHO FELL TO EARTH
Walter Tevis
1963

"An air of melancholy permeates..."

With the success of the Netflix series **The Queen's Gambit** based on a novel by Walter Tevis, there has been a resurgence in interest in his works. I thought this would be the perfect time to reread his first science fiction novel, *The Man Who Fell to Earth*. The novel begins with Thomas Newton selling a gold ring at a pawn shop. He has hundreds of them and will use the money that he raises selling them to hire patent attorney Oliver Farnsworth. Newton is an alien from the planet Anthea, and, with Farnsworth's help, he will use the scientific information that he brought with him to build a fortune so that he can build a spaceship to return with water to help his drought-ridden, dying planet. An air of melancholy permeates the book. Gravity, both literally and figuratively, presses down on Newton, as he deals with his longing for his wife and planet

FROM OUTER SPACE

Avon Books retitled *Needle* as *From Outer Space* for the first paperback edition, presumably to suggest a connection to the movies such as *It Came From Outer Space*. Although probably not *Plan 9 From Outer Space*. Cover by Richard Powers.

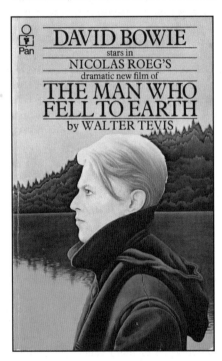

THE MAN WHO FELL TO EARTH

What makes this 1976 UK Pan Books movie tie-in so interesting, is that the cover painting of David Bowie is by George Underwood, who played in a band with Bowie whilst at art school and remained a life-long friend.

AVON
35¢
T-175

"Exciting science fiction, absolutely unique"
—*Montgomery Advertiser*

From Outer Space

Hal Clement

Complete and Unabridged
Originally published as NEEDLE by Doubleday & Co., Inc.

through drinking. There is also a film version directed by Nicholas Roeg, starring David Bowie. I need to revisit this as well, as I have not seen it in over 30 years, but I remember it as being a very faithful adaptation, with Bowie providing an outstanding performance as Newton. If you remove the alien from the book, it is amazing how prescient this novel is. Large corporations like Kodak, that we always thought would be around forever, are side-lined by disruptive new technologies, and billionaires build their own private space programs. But the big difference is that Thomas Newton seems more human than our real-life space-traveling billionaires. This reader empathized with Newton, which I don't find myself doing with Bezos, Musk or Branson.

Tom Tesarek

✵ ✵ ✵ ✵

MICHAEL KANE 1: CITY OF THE BEAST
Michael Moorcock
1965

"A young Moorcock nails the atmosphere of adventure and an exotic world..."

"I went to Mars ... an older Mars, eons in the past, yet still ancient ... I encountered a strange romantic civilization totally unlike any we have ever had on Earth ... And there was a girl, young, ravishingly attractive. She was Princess of Varnal, City of the Green Mists, with its spires and colonnades, its strong, slender people – and the finest fighting men in the martial world ..." So begin the adventures of Michael Kane, Vietnam veteran and scientist who invents a matter transmitter and gets accidently sent to the Red Planet. In 1964, at the start of a career which should last 6 decades and counting, Michael Moorcock wrote this short novel and its two sequels under the pen-name Edward P. Bradbury. Having produced a fanzine called Burroughsania in his youth the writer later reported: "I wrote the whole series in just over a week and tired, but happy, expected them to come and go and be forgotten about almost as soon as they were published." But they were not, and while the claim is a bit dubious considering the overall length of the trilogy, this remains a well-written Burroughs pastiche. Surely it doesn't re-invent as much as it follows the formula, but young Moorcock nails the atmosphere of adventure and an exotic world. This is still a fast read; it is the little things which are fun from a contemporary view; for once it makes sense that

the hero is a superb swordsman, and the princess doesn't fall for him first. The DAW covers by Richard Hescox are as good as the earlier British ones by Richard Clifton-Day - see overleaf. Andreas Decker

✵ ✵ ✵

NEEDLE
Hal Clement
1950

"A fun read with very relatable characters ..."

Even in space, there is still a need for authority to neutralize criminals. What happens when an interstellar bad guy escapes to a backwater planet known as Earth? Needle follows the Hunter, as he crashes in the Pacific Ocean chasing his Quarry. Hunter must safely arrive on a nearby island and then contact the bipedal aliens that make up the civilization of this world. How will Hunter locate the Quarry, especially since they are both three-pound symbiotic jellies that live inside oxygen breathing hosts? After finding teenager Bob Kinnaird asleep on the beach, Hunter oozes in and sets up shop, spreading himself through Bob's body so he can see out of Bob's eyes and hear with Bob's ears. Bob returns to his boarding school in Boston, so it's Hunter's chance to learn English, how to read, and ponder how to let Bob know he's been carrying an alien around inside. Take over the vocal cords to try and croak out some words? Bad idea. Start tapping Bob's fingers in Morse Code? Nope! Hunter finally manipulates Bob's retinas to create written subtitles. Now, all Hunter needs to do is get out there to find the Quarry, who could be hiding in any living animal – like finding a needle in a haystack. Originally serialized in Astounding in 1949, Needle is a fun read with very relatable characters. You get to watch Hunter and Bob solve problems, create a list of possible suspects and pick up the cold trail of the Quarry. I've really enjoyed reading *Needle* and it is a great science fiction mystery!

Penny Tesarek

✵ ✵ ✵ ✵ ✵

FANTASTIC FACTOID 3

MOORCOCK ON MARS

PSEUDONYMOUS WORK BY MICHAEL MOORCOCK BECOMES AMONGST HIS MOST REPRINTED WORKS

In 1965, Michael Moorcock was working at UK publisher Compact, editing and writing SF magazines. A life-long fan of Edgar Rice Burroughs, Moorcock produced a trilogy of well-done but disposable ERB pastiches in the form of the Michael Kane series as by Edward P Bradbury: Warriors of Mars, Blades of Mars and Barbarians of Mars. They appeared in 1965 at Compact with painted covers by his good friend James Cawthorn, whom he had met whilst producing ERB-zines in the UK. Cawthorn would go on to produce graphic novels based on Moorcock's HAWKMOON series. Moorcock may have expected the books to have disappeared without trace, but they have gone on to multiple printings across the world, with some excellent covers. At some point, *Warriors* was renamed *City of the Beast*, *Blades* as *Lord of the Spiders*, and *Barbarians* as *Masters of the Pit*. Michael Kane was even featured as a character in the Mars sequence of the famous LEAGUE OF EXTRAORDINARY GENTLEMEN comic book. Not bad for a series of written-for-the-fun pastiches.

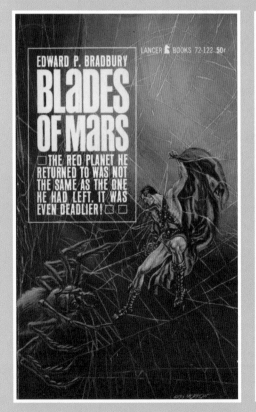

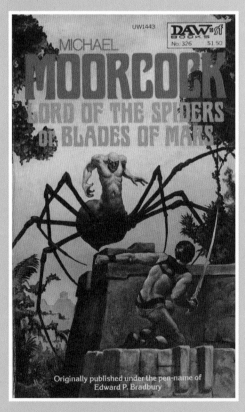

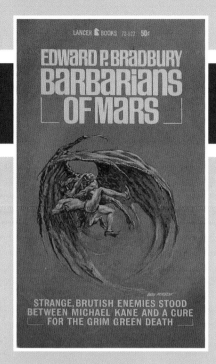

EDWARD P. BRADBURY
**BARBARIANS
OF MARS**

LANCER BOOKS 72-127 50¢

STRANGE, BRUTISH ENEMIES STOOD
BETWEEN MICHAEL KANE AND A CURE
FOR THE GRIM GREEN DEATH

NEW ENGLISH LIBRARY
**Michael
Moorcock**
MASTERS OF THE PIT

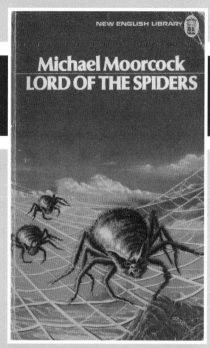

NEW ENGLISH LIBRARY
**Michael Moorcock
LORD OF THE SPIDERS**

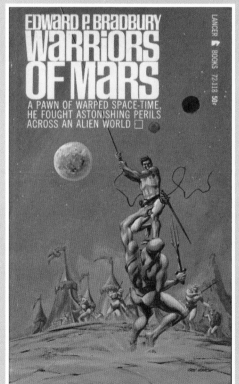

EDWARD P. BRADBURY
**WARRIORS
OF MARS**

LANCER BOOKS 72-118 50¢

A PAWN OF WARPED SPACE-TIME,
HE FOUGHT ASTONISHING PERILS
ACROSS AN ALIEN WORLD

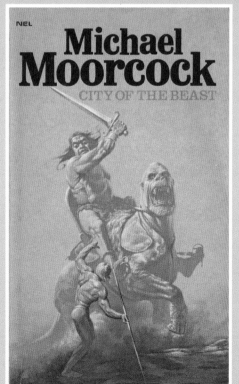

NEL
**Michael
Moorcock**
CITY OF THE BEAST

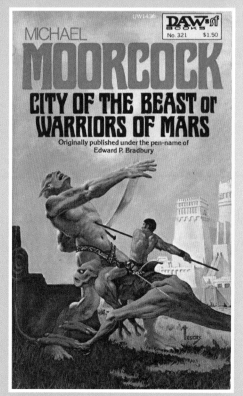

UW1436
DAW BOOKS
No. 321 $1.50

MICHAEL
MOORCOCK
**CITY OF THE BEAST or
WARRIORS OF MARS**
Originally published under the pen-name of
Edward P. Bradbury

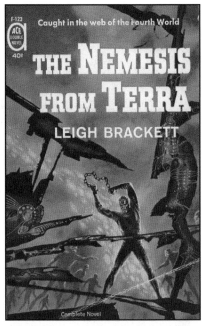

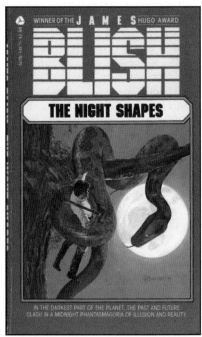

THE NEMESIS FROM TERRA
Leigh Brackett
1961

"Long on plot and short on world or character building..."

Leigh Brackett was a well-known and prolific author of science fiction short stories and novels from the pulp era as well as a screen writer. Much of her work is of the "planetary adventure" or "planetary romance" variety and this one sort of falls into that category. Often referred to as the "Queen of Space Opera", she wrote in what was the consensus Mars world of science fiction from the 1930s to the 1950s, so world-building as we know it today in Sci-Fi was not as necessary. The novel opens with Rick Urquhart attempting to evade "The Company", a rather ruthless mining conglomerate that wields much power on Mars. Tension has been building between rebellious Martians and humans who work for The Company. Rick encounters a Martian who prophesizes that Rick will ultimately rule the planet. Unfortunately, The Company catches Rick and sends him back to labour in the mines once again. From there the story takes off in a series of adventures involving his escape, a Martian-rights activist/love interest, travel to the Martian North Pole to meet with the "Thinkers", overcoming several power-hungry bad guys, capture by the Martians, and ultimately rising to become the Martian's greatest hope for success. That's a lot of plot to cover in one relatively slender book. It is typical of the era as it is long on plot and short on world or character building. The style of this one is reflective of Brackett's previous work on a crime-noir novel and is darker than most of her later work which morphed into a more fluid style. I'm glad I read this one, even if it isn't a perfect representative sample of her work.
Benjamin Thomas

THE NIGHT SHAPES
James Blish
1962

"A vivid enough creation in a pulp kind of way ..."

Blish was an interesting writer in that he was able to straddle the worlds of commercially driven writing (**Star Trek** novelisations) and more cerebral writing (Hugo-award and Nebula-nominations), albeit never with the same book. As a fan of his excellent satanic SF/anti-nuclear weapon *Black Easter* and also of dinosaurs (no bigger plot spoiler than the cover illustration of the UK Four Square edition I own) this book was a real disappointment. It is a fix-up of two pulp shorts which originally appeared in late 1940s issues of **Jungle Stories**, so it works as a jungle-adventure story set in an Africa which modern readers wouldn't recognise, and lacks the nuance of Blish's best work. There is only the most fleeting, albeit important, appearance of the legendary "Mokele-mbembe", so it is lacking on the dinosaur front and other fantasy elements. Lead character Kennedy is a white American who has given it all up to be an explorer in Africa and now despises American culture. He is a vivid enough creation in a pulp kind of way, as is the vivacious wife of one of his party whose blouse is consistently under threat by her breasts, the jungle vegetation, and a growing sexual tension with Kennedy. There is one excellent sequence where Kennedy is in the grip of a constricting python which does generate some tension from a hackneyed scenario. Best categorised as a fossil.
Justin Marriott

NIGHT SHAPES 1963 UK Four Square edition with a cover that is something of a plot spoiler. Although uncredited, it is possible the work of Josh Kirby.

NEMESIS FROM TERRA 1961 Ace Books edition of *Shadow Over Mars*, with a suitably moody Ed Emshwiller cover for a neo-crime SF.

NIGHT SHAPES Avon Book's cover for a 1983 reprint shows the best scene from the book, although it is crudely executed. Although signed, I don't recognise the signature of the artist.

NIGHT WALK
Bob Shaw
1967

"Inventive, busy and with a deft turn of phrase ..."

A cold-war thriller set on the planet of Emm Luther, a rival to Earth in the pursuit of a new planet to colonise as a fix for over-population issues. Tensions are running hot between Earth and Emm Luther, so when human spy Tallon is caught, he is blinded and thrown into a prison which is surrounded by a swamp full of hungry critters. With a device that allows him to see through the eyes of others, including at various points a bird of prey and a small dog, Tallon escapes and goes on the run, hoping other Earth spies rescue him before the Emm Luther secret police catch up with him. I was really taken aback at just how hardboiled and exciting this story was, especially in comparison with much of the straight spy fiction of that era. Tallon is a perfect spy; resourceful, intelligent and cold-blooded. Beyond a sardonic humour, he is lacking in some human qualities, which may have made him a more sympathetic character (at one point he seriously beats a defenceless woman who had entrapped him). I was also surprised at how many locations the book visited, as I had assumed it to be mainly set in the swamp. Although that sequence was thrilling as three prisoners are assailed by voracious creatures, with only Tallon surviving. I did find the Cold War style politics over-simple, in that both Earth and Emm Luther's motives are equally selfish, but the Emm Lutherians are clearly the villains of the piece, albeit Tallon does turn on his employees at the finale. Shaw is an excellent writer, inventive, busy and with a deft turn of phrase, and I will be seeking out more of his works.

Justin Marriott

⚛ ⚛ ⚛

OPEN PRISON
James White
1964

"Too preachy for my tastes..."

An uneven mix of philosophy and military-SF, as author White reimagines *Lord of the Flies* with the warring tribes made up of human prisoners of war dumped by a race nicknamed the "bugs" on a penal planet with an Earth-like climate. There are no guards or cells, so the prisoners are free to follow their will, splitting into two groups with opposing philosophies; one adopting a hippy outlook where they focus on building a new life on the planet, whilst the other maintain their military uniforms and rank whilst plotting how to escape and wage war. When a new batch of prisoners are dropped on the planet, they must navigate their way through the politics and violence of their new prison home. This is a contradictory book, both pessimistic and optimistic about the nature of man, and featuring a strong female lead yet constantly making reference to her looks. Reference works state it reflects White's pacifist philosophy, and maybe it is anti-military compared to Robert A Heinlein's works of that era, but it didn't strike me as especially pacifist with all of the characters military personnel and dealing with heroic tropes. White is a great ideas man, with his series of SF stories set in an interplanetary hospital springing to mind, and I can see how certain elements of *Open Prison* may have been looted for the *Starship Troopers* film, but his writing style is too preachy for my tastes, and he spells everything out for the reader in painfully long exposition.

Justin Marriott

⚛ ⚛

PAINGOD
Harlan Ellison
1965

"Overwritten and over-wrought, but also brilliant and ingenious..."

A seven-handed collection of Ellison's short stories, all previously published in SF digests, with over half farmed from

---

NIGHT WALK UK New English Library 1970 edition of Shaw's spy/action-adventure SF title. Art uncredited but probably George Underwood.

OPEN PRISON UK Four Square 1965 edition of White's unfulfilling military SF. Another uncredited cover, but likely to be Josh Kirby.

PAINGOD 1969 Pyramid collection of Ellison shorts, which reconstituted Jack Gaughan's artwork from the first edition in 1965.

NEL 2641 NEW ENGLISH LIBRARY SCIENCE-FICTION

Bob Shaw
Night Walk

A FOUR SQUARE BOOK   3'6

OPEN PRISON
JAMES WHITE

They planned the biggest
prison escape the
Galaxy had ever seen!

PYRAMID SCIENCE FICTION X-1991 60c
HARLAN ELLISON
Seven soul-shuddering treks
through a universe of thoughts
never thought before
PAINGOD
and Other Delusions

PLANET OF THE APES ISSUE 13 ORIGINAL ART BY BOB LARKIN
Larkin provided a typically eye-catching image for Marvel's black and white magazine, illustrating a scene from 'The Magick-Man's Last Gasp Purple Light Show'. Pretentious, Moi?

RETIEF'S WAR
The third Retief novel appeared in paperback in 1967, courtesy of Berkely Books, with a Richard Powers cover. The story had originally run over 3 parts in IF magazine in late 1965.

recent (at the time) publications. All the stories include trademark Ellison introductions, albeit shorter than his 70s examples, which are consistently enlightening and entertaining. The short stories are archetypal Ellison material, tending to be overwritten and over-wrought (the anthologies theme is pain) but also brilliant and ingenious. Beyond his classic 'Repent Harlequin Said the Ticktockman', the pick of the bunch was the titular 'Paingod' in which the creature selected to be the entity deciding how and to whom pain is allocated, gets too close to his subjects (obvious ending yet wonderful characterisation) and 'The Discards' about the mutants forced off earth and now live in an orbiting spaceship (clunky yet compelling). Unlikely to convert you if you are not currently an Ellison-maniac, a very diverting collection if you have a propensity for Ellison. I am the former, hence the stingy rating.
Justin Marriott

PLANET OF THE APES MAGAZINE
1974-77

"The only good human is a dead human..."

How can I ever forget watching it on the living room floor in my onesie with that itchy gold shag carpet before I almost swallowed my pacifier as that creepy ram horn blows and the humans start running...thanks for watching over me mom? Riding on the great success of the hit movie franchise, Marvel Comics' **Planet of the Apes** magazine was published under their Curtis imprint from 1974-1977 as part of their new black-and-white magazine series. It has a special place in many young fans hearts since it was the first ongoing comic book series related to the **Planet of the Apes** franchise. It was also the first medium to introduce new original **Planet of the Apes** material set in a variety of different regions, eras and conditions that had never been seen before (or since), beginning with a non-continuity serial entitled **Terror on the Planet of the Apes**. (Marvel also published the **Adventures of the Planet of the Apes** colour comic adapting the first two films over eleven issues.) One of Marvel's best writers Doug Moench wrote these new imaginary tales for the twenty-nine issue run with some dynamic Mike Ploog and Tom Sutton interior artwork. But the real draw for me and many others were those fantastic full colour covers! These painted gems were provided by the likes of artists Earl Norem, Gray Morrow, Ken Barr, Bob Larkin, and

Malcolm McNeill. Used for the American series a group of the best were also reprinted for the **Planet of the Apes** series published in England. Remember the only good human is a dead human!
Dave Karlen

RETIEF'S WAR
Keith Laumer
1978

"Humour is its strongest characteristic..."

Laumer creates worlds that are outrageously fun and then brings in Retief, a clever diplomat known for going rogue from the established procedures of a diplomat that manages to save the day and weasels his way out of trouble while somehow making his superiors look good. At times, Retief will remind the reader of a James Bond type character in a futuristic Science Fiction setting. The main source of humour springs from the wildly imaginative (and quite improbable) inhabitants of the planet Quoop. Somehow these people have evolved into a mix of mechanical people with wheels instead of legs and sharp talons. The birds don't have wings, but instead are more like helicopters with rotors to provide lift. Their commentary and backwards customs bring a smile to the reader's face. An earthling is known as a Terry, short for terrestrial, and mocked for having legs instead of wheels. The Quoopians don't understand how Retief can get along on his legs and call him a "stilter." Retief is forced to disguise himself as one of them by having a mechanical costume built so he can go among them unrecognized as a Terry. Retief spots a plot to subjugate the planet under one of the tribes, a group of ne'er-do-wells who immediately seize power. Our hero takes it upon himself to wander about and inciting the other tribes to unite against the tyrannical power and the diplomatic plot to subjugate them. He finds himself in tight spot after tight spot and uses some of his diplomatic training and some of his James Bond-like tricks. Before long, the planet is in an uproar as the tyrants, armed with actual weapons, continue their effort of subjugation. Retief becomes their leader and teaches them some military tactics. Some of those tactics are hilarious as the reader strives to picture these wheeled creatures getting bogged down in mud or knocked over like a tortoise flipped over on its shell. There is nothing ground-breaking or especially exciting in regard to

MARVEL COMICS CALLED ON SOME OF THE BEST IN THE INDUSTRY TO PROVIDE A GALLERY OF THE APES

Marvel Comics put some of their very best cover painters to work on this high-quality tie-in to the movie and TV series franchise, which contained some excellent strips written by Doug Moench and illustrated by Tom Sutton and Mike Ploog. Cover artists included-

BOB LARKIN (issue 15 and 19) provided covers which no Apes movie could possibly replicate, with the underwater ape vs squid an especially wild image.

EARL NOREM (issue 21) had cut his teeth in the Men's Adventure Mags, so there was always an element of sleazy titillation to his images. He found much work on SAVAGE SWORD OF CONAN covers.

GRAY MORROW (issue 11) was a classic illustrator whose Marvel career was sporadic.

GREG THEAKSTON (issue 9) went on to success in paperback illustration, but his early cover work at Marvel was often repainted and his work dried up at the publishers.

KEN BARR (issue 18) provided his trademark dazzling colours, although the gorilla had been too exaggerated, presumably at the behest of an art editor looking for sensationalism.

MALCOLM MCNEILL (14 and 26) was credited as Malcolm McN for reasons I do not know. His apes as Vikings image is a classic and far superior to the internal Herb Trimpe illustrations on 'North Lands!'

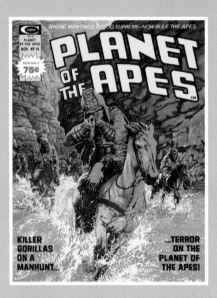

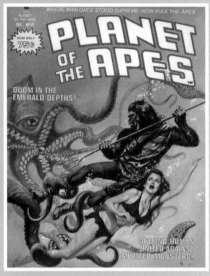

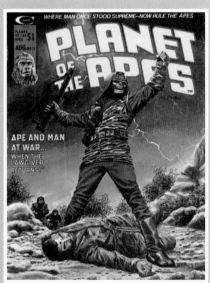

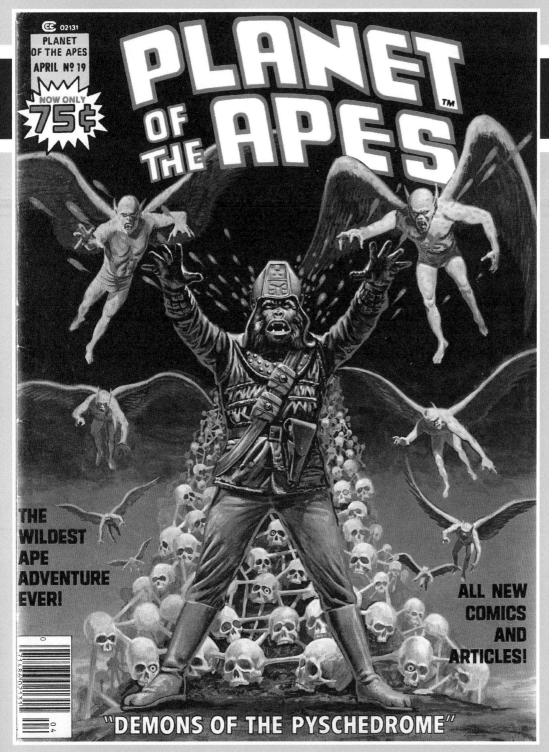

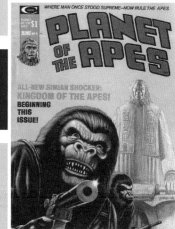

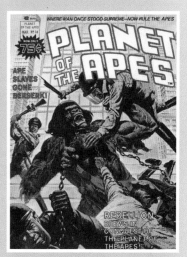

Science Fiction as the author chooses to play this one for laughs. The novel seems to be almost a parody of the geopolitical structure of our world during the cold war. The novel isn't a long one but ends at just the right moment. The humour is its strongest characteristic with its implied political commentary coming in a close second place.

David "the preacher" Wilson

⚛ ⚛

THE RIM OF THE UNKNOWN
Frank Belknap Long
1978 edition

"A psychiatrist could have a field day with the sexual imagery..."

A paperback reprint by the short-lived Condor line of an Arkham House hardback which collected three stories by Long from 30s pulps, set in a future where humans have been reduced in size (or live with the threat of being reduced in size) whilst insects and molluscs have evolved super-intelligence and grown to massive size. The land is ruled by warring factions of ants and bees, whilst molluscs rule the sea but plan to take over the land as well. Humans are kept as servants and, in the case of those serving the molluscs, genetically modified –for instance being given webbed feet– so as to become more adept at their jobs. Despite their absurd premise, the three stories carry an emotional impact and pathos which totally caught me by surprise. It's difficult to put my finger on quite why this is. Certainly, Long displays his human characters as noble and principled, showing a bravery we all wish we would show when faced with adversity. The three stories also touch on the very nature of what it is to be a human, by contrasting the hive mentality of the insects with the yearning for personal freedom, so again Long may be touching on primordial emotions. I'm sure a psychiatrist could have a field day with the sexual imagery and insecurities Long's portrays, especially his obsession with size and men being shrunk so they can no longer satisfy their mate. Long's style of writing in this trio is different to his typical work, using language that is far denser and more baroque than I had previously encountered in his stories, almost a pastiche of Clark Ashton Smith's unique style. He had also evidently invested time in creating his bizarre future scenario, where strange insect inventions and customs abound, so I believe these were

far more personally significant to him than other hack work of that period. I see these as Long's equivalent of a Cthulhu mythos, his attempt to create his own universe with the Barnacle Masters as his elder gods.

Justin Marriott

⚛ ⚛ ⚛

THE RITUALS OF INFINITY
Michael Morrocock
1971

"The strangely optimistic end is surreal, bombastic and fun..."

There are fifteen planets Earth in subspace, but it used to be twenty-four or more. The unknown D-squads are destroying one after the other. Professor Faustaff from Earth-1 and his men are fighting against the faceless attackers, voyaging through dimensional tunnels from planet Earth to planet Earth in a race against time. But now Faustaff meets for the first time the Principals, the creators of all those worlds. And he has to ask himself what is real and what is not, humanity included. Originally a 3-part serial in the magazine **New Worlds** in 1965 under the title *The Wrecks of Time* – which is the current eBook title – this is one of Moorcock's early sf novels. It begins with a flamboyant scene which in hindsight is so typical for its time: Professor Falstaff, six and a half feet and weighing 20 stone, clad in a Hawaiian shirt and shorts, driving in a flame-red Buick through the American desert to San Francisco on Earth-3, taking beautiful hitch-hiker Nancy with him. In the background you seem to hear The Rolling Stones doing the soundtrack. The idea of parallel earths had already been done before the 60s, but here Moorcock developed the concept further, and his fans will recognize a lot of ideas he later re-used, right down to a crucified man. This fix-up novel version is a short read, no ounce of fat on its narrative bones, and while the characterisation may be a bit shallow, the strangely optimistic end is surreal, bombastic and fun.

Andreas Decker

⚛ ⚛ ⚛

RIM OF THE UNKNOWN

Condor were a short-lived late 70s publishing house. This was their reprint of an interesting Arkham House collection with a new cover by Ken Barr.

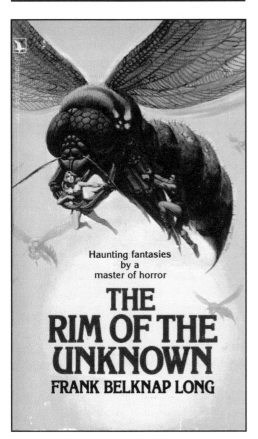

Haunting fantasies
by a
master of horror

THE RIM OF THE UNKNOWN

FRANK BELKNAP LONG

THE WRECKS OF TIME

This was the original version of *The Rituals of Infinity*, which was published in three episodes across the Michael Moorcock edited NEW WORLDS. Hence the James Colvin pseudonym. This November 1965 also featured a short story by Terry Pratchett.

NEW WORLDS

Ⓒ COMPACT SF

2/6

JAMES COLVIN's

The WRECKS of TIME

Two strange men struggled over the fate of the bizarre worlds of subspace

ROADMARKS

1981 UK edition that gives good dragon courtesy of Tim White. White's colour were always vibrant, and he also experimented with using clay models on his covers which gave them a distinctive look.

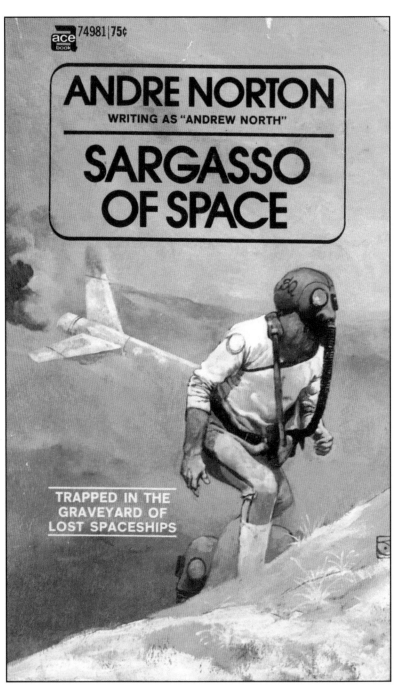

ace book 74981|75¢

ANDRE NORTON
WRITING AS "ANDREW NORTH"

SARGASSO OF SPACE

TRAPPED IN THE GRAVEYARD OF LOST SPACESHIPS

SARGASSO OF SPACE

Sargasso first appeared in hardback at Gnome Press as by Andrew North. It went through multiple paperback editions at Ace, including this one where Catherine Jeffrey Jones use of a WWI style gasmask gives an early steampunk feel.

ROADMARKS
Roger Zelazny
1979

"He uses it to throw in everything but the kitchen sink..."

Red Dorakeen travels the Road searching for a time and place that he has left behind. On the Road, one can travel into the past or the future, as well as alternate timelines where events happened differently. One of Red's enemies has declared a Black Decade, which by the rules of the Road means that he has ten attempts to take Red's life, using assassins taken from both the past and the future. Helping Red to avoid this fate is his AI (artificial intelligence) that has the appearance of the poetry book *Flowers of Evil* by Baudelaire. With this premise Zelazny weaves an entertaining tale. While the Road resembles the Pattern in his Amber stories, here he uses it to throw in everything but the kitchen sink. Dragons? Check. Guest appearances by Hitler and the Marquis de Sade? Check. A telepathically controlled T Rex? Hell yes! Unfortunately, Zelazny loses points for succumbing to one of my personal pet peeves-he includes the poetry in the original French, without providing any translation. I admit that I am an ignorant American who doesn't speak fluent French, but you don't need to rub my nose in it! While I wouldn't include this in the list of Zelazny's best books, it is a quick read that is quite a bit of fun. Well worth your time.

Tom Tesarek

SARGASSO OF SPACE
Andre Norton
1955

"Exactly the right decision on Norton's part to make ... the novel to work as an adventure story..."

The main character here is Apprentice Cargo-Master Dane Thorson, who is reporting to his first assignment aboard The Solar Queen, a small independent merchant ship. He's soon off on his first journey into space when the Queen takes off to deliver a team of scientists to a newly discovered planet. Soon, though, there are reasons to believe the scientists are not scientists. There are wrecked spaceships--some of them centuries or even millennia old--all over the place, and a mysterious force prevents the Queen from taking off again after

landing on the planet. A crew member goes missing and a band of armed men surround the Queen and demand its surrender. Dane is our point-of-view character. He makes a few rookie mistakes but performs intelligently and contributes to the eventual good-guy victory. But he's still the newest and least experienced member of the crew and Norton makes no effort to artificially thrust him into "the hero who saves the day" mode. He's one part of a team. This is exactly the right decision on Norton's part to make Dane work as a character and for the novel to work as an adventure story. It allows us to believe that the Solar Queen is a real ship that functions successfully because the entire crew is competent. It makes for a great start to a series of books that will eventually bring Dane into the captain's seat.

Tim Deforest

SOLDIER, ASK NOT
Gordon R. Dickson
1964

"The novel's dark overtone carries the reader to the conclusion in a sense of sorrow and bewilderment..."

When humans settle the stars, they splinter into three philosophical groups, choosing to follow religious fanaticism or military strength or a quest for knowledge. Soon, the three groups are living in their respective planetary systems in a see-saw between harmony and war. Into this tense situation comes Tam, a young newsman. Tam visits "The Encyclopaedia", an overblown version of the internet designed to combine all of the information man has ever known. There he has a mental experience that opens his mind and permits him to be able to perceive details and postulate outcomes, etc. This experience causes those who run the program to believe that he will either save humanity or destroy it. He refuses to participate, despite their repeated overtures to him, choosing to use his mental abilities for selfish purposes. Tam grows to learn how the Encyclopaedia program might just save humankind. This novel is dark and brooding, the author uses a lot of scenes set in falling rain to help set the mood. There is some action that breaks the stark mood, but not enough to elevate this novel to anything exciting. Instead, the novel's dark overtone carries the reader to the conclusion in a sense of sorrow and bewilderment. Overall, the novel offers an interesting look at

FANTASTIC FACTOID 5

NORTON and BARR

ANDRE NORTON'S PAPERBACKS WERE TEAMED UP BY FAWCETT WITH KEN BARR PAINTINGS FOR A SERIES OF STRIKING NEW EDITIONS

Andre Norton's career spanned six decades, and her stories of unknown planets, time travel and Witch World have constantly been in print. US publisher Fawcett made a concerted effort to provide her books with glossy and updated packaging in 1979. They combined a well-designed logo of her name (which would be further tweaked) and a series of paintings by Ken Barr.

Barr was a Scotsman who started in war comics in Scotland, but emigrated to the US where he worked at DC (also on war comics) before his work started to be picked up by paperback publishers and comic magazines from Marvel and Warren. Across these two pages are examples of the reissued paperbacks.

The original art to the right is from *The X-Factor* edition published in 1981.

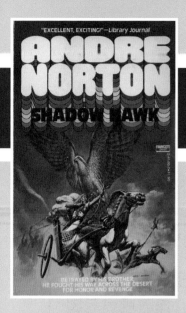

"EXCELLENT, EXCITING!"—Library Journal

ANDRE NORTON

SHADOW HAWK

BETRAYED BY HIS BROTHER,
HE FOUGHT HIS WAY ACROSS THE DESERT
FOR HONOR AND REVENGE

Author of JUDGMENT ON JANUS

ANDRE NORTON

VICTORY ON JANUS

PART HUMAN, PART IFTIN,
THE CHANGELINGS OF JANUS
NOW FACED SECRET DESTROYERS
HIDDEN BEHIND THE MASK OF
BROTHERLY LOVE.

ANDRE NORTON

POSTMARKED THE STARS

IN THE WILD ZONES OF SPACE,
ONLY COURAGE ENDURES...

Author of JUDGMENT ON JANUS

ANDRE NORTON

SEA SIEGE

"IMAGINATIVE, COMPELLING SCIENCE FICTION"
—Booklist

THE DEADLY WAR
WAS OVER
—BUT THE SEAS
OF THE WORLD
WERE INFESTED
WITH A TERROR
THAT HAD ONLY
JUST BEGUN...

ANDRE NORTON

HUON OF THE HORN

A wondrous
tale of brave knights,
black-hearted villains, and
fairy kings in a magical time
of the long ago.

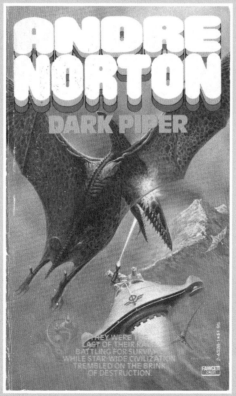

ANDRE NORTON

DARK PIPER

THEY WERE
LAST OF THEIR KIND,
BATTLING FOR SURVIVAL
WHILE STAR-WIDE CIVILIZATION
TREMBLED ON THE BRINK
OF DESTRUCTION.

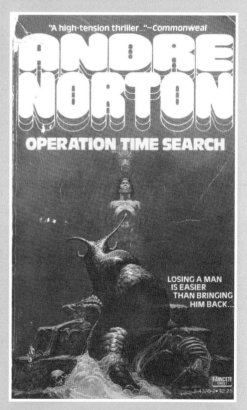

"A high-tension thriller..."—Commonweal

ANDRE NORTON

OPERATION TIME SEARCH

LOSING A MAN
IS EASIER
THAN BRINGING
HIM BACK...

a bleak future, which is not hopeless, but offers difficulties for humankind to overcome. Some of those difficulties reflect some we face today in our segmented political society as the right and the left in American politics jostle for power. The novel suggests that Tam is the focal point for change and resolution but concludes with the only resolution being in his own point of view. Will he be the catalyst foreseen by the exotic faction that will push humanity towards the next evolutionary step? While the reader might be satisfied knowing that the hero could change his way of thinking and might be the necessary salvation for humankind, he might also share my feelings that the resolution is sorely lacking. I know that the author wrote more stories set in this universe, perhaps the most well-known is the **Dorsai** series. This volume introduced me to that universe and there are probably a few crossover characters, but the lack of action and the bleak outlook doesn't exactly make me want to catch up on this corner of Dickson's literary universe.

David "the preacher" Wilson

⚛ ⚛ ⚛

SPACE CAPTAIN
Murrey Leinster
1966

"Takes that genre and shows us how to do it right ..."

Captain Trent, who has just been hired to command the space freighter Yarrow, comes from a long line of space captains--and before that sea captains. Swashbuckling seems to be genetically encoded in his family line. And, by golly, he'll need to buckle quite a few swashes. The Yarrow is going to attempt to reopen trade with a group of planets who have been plagued with space piracy so intense that interplanetary trade has pretty much shut down. The novel is enormously fun, following along after Captain Trent as he plots for ways to use his unarmed ship to fight armed pirate vessels. The story can be very roughly divided into three acts. Act One has Trent damaging a pirate ship and forcing it to retreat by just ramming it. Act Two involves luring some pirates aboard a derelict spaceship, then ambushing them. The pirate ship itself gets away, but Trent can bring a number of prisoners to a nearby planet. In the final act, Trent figures out where the pirate base is and takes his ship there. Remember that the Yarrow isn't armed, so a ground assault will be necessary to wipe out the pirates

and rescue hostages. *Space Captain* is Space Opera done right, with the reader taken to far-away stars to battle and out-smart ruthless villains. It does not break any new ground in the genre--it simply takes that genre and shows us how to do it right.

Tim Deforest

⚛ ⚛ ⚛ ⚛

SPACIAL DELIVERY
Gordon Dickson
1961

"Keeps the reader turning pages and wishing that the story could go just a bit longer..."

"Spacial" Delivery is a hilarious read and well worth the reader's time if they are into Science Fiction humour. In this case, a former Olympic athlete is drafted by the diplomatic corps and given an assignment with the briefest of briefings. Off he goes with the assignment to settle a dispute on a planet of large bear-like creatures. The only way to get him across the countryside is in the pack of the huge bearish mail carrier. (Get it-- the mail carrier became a male carrier?) As if being carried about in a pack of this huge carrier doesn't provide adequate humour, he soon discovers that he has been summoned to FIGHT one of the giant bear creatures. While this short Science Fiction novel that isn't especially heavy on Science Fiction, it offers enough comical moments. It is packed with a number of classic Science-Fiction counter-cultural ideas.

SPACE CAPTIAN
Part of an Ace Double in 1966, the story was first published across two parts as Killer Ship in AMAZING STORIES in 1965. Gray Morrow cover art.

SPACIAL DELIVERY
Half of an Ace Double in 1961, with a cover by Ed Emshwiller.

SOLDIER, ASK NOT
1975 DAW Books edition with a Kelly Freas cover. As a short story in a 1964 issue of GALAXY, it won a Hugo Award.

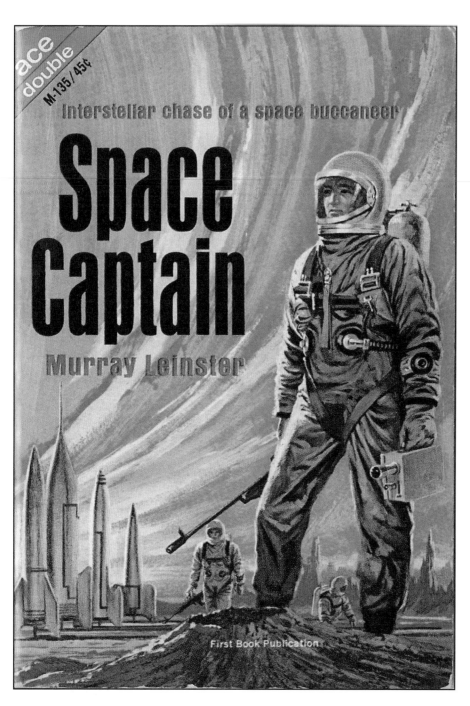

ace double

M-135/45¢

Interstellar chase of a space buccaneer

Space Captain

Murray Leinster

First Book Publication

F-119

ace double novel

40¢

Rendezvous with a double-sized Goliath

SPACIAL DELIVERY

GORDON R. DICKSON

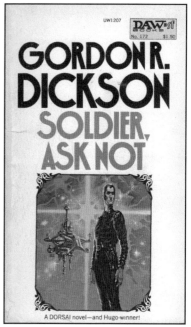

UW1207
DAW BOOKS
No. 172 $1.50

GORDON R. DICKSON
SOLDIER, ASK NOT

A DORSAI novel—and Hugo-winner!

A monster attack leaves Captain Kirk
mentally unfit to command the Enterprise!

Dickson keeps the story moving rapidly and the novel is short enough to finish quickly. His style moves along at a brisk clip yet never seems rushed. The comic moments and the frantic pace keeps the reader turning pages and wishing that the story could go just a bit longer.

David "the preacher" Wilson

⚛ ⚛ ⚛ ⚛

STAND BY FOR MARS!
Carey Rockwell
1952

"Emphasis on the necessity of teamwork and the need to think and act intelligently..."

The first of eight novels based on the early SF TV series **Tom Corbett, Space Cadet**, the novel covers Tom's first few months at the Space Academy. In terms of characterization, it's fairly straightforward--Tom is a straight-arrow guy who wants to do well. One of his teammates (cadets are assigned to teams of three) is Roger Manning, who is brilliant but snotty and disrespectful. The third team member is Astro, who is already a skilled engineer but struggles with the advanced mathematics he must learn. The intelligence and education of the three cadets is continually emphasized. At one point, when Roger talks about doing logarithms in his head when no computer is available, you want to smack him one for being such a smarty-pants. But you don't doubt for a moment that he can do it. It isn't long before we get to the action, though.

STAR TREK ORIGINAL ART
George Wilson was hugely prolific as a cover painter for Gold Key comics who specialised in tie-ins to TV series or characters. This is his art for issue 50 of their STAR TREK tie-in from 1978, which ran long after the TV series finished.

STAR TREK
May 1972 issue with Wilson illustrating 'The Enterprise Mutiny'.

STAND BY FOR MARS!
1952 hardback, published to tie-in with the popularity of the radio show.

While out on training manoeuvres, Tom's ship answers a distress signal. What follows in quick succession are rescuing passengers off a damaged ship before it blows up; doing make-shift repairs on the ship; crash-landing in the Martian desert; surviving a three-day sandstorm; digging their way out of the wrecked ship without drowning in powdery sand; and walking across the blistering hot desert with insufficient water. It's well-told and exciting stuff, with the emphasis on the necessity of teamwork and the need to think and act intelligently. Everything Tom and his team do makes sense, as they take carefully calculated risks before acting to first save others and then save themselves.

Tim Deforest

⚛ ⚛ ⚛

STAR TREK
61 issues, 1967-79
Gold Key Comics

"Which might explain the flames shooting out of the Enterprise engines on some of the pages ..."

I can still hear the opening music now in my head... Space, the final frontier...SWOOSH goes the ship...well you know the rest. One of the many licensed properties that Gold Key Comics published in the late 1960s was NBC's new science fiction television show, **Star Trek**. Even though the program only lasted three years before cancellation, its success in reruns helped promote this first **Star Trek** comic series which debuted in September of 1967 and lasted for thirteen years. Italian artist Giovanni Ticci drew the first issue followed by Nevio Zeccara for the second in his loose cartoony style, before fan favourite Alberto Giolitti took over the pencilling with the help of his studio for the next ten years. With just a handful of stories based on the original TV series, the writers and artists at Gold Key created bold new adventures for Captain Kirk, Mr. Spock, Dr. McCoy, and the valiant crew of the Starship Enterprise. Gerry Boudreau, Arnold Drake, and Len Wein were just some of the talented writers to work on the feature, showcasing Giolitti's exciting aliens, savage landscapes, and weird architecture before the artist eventually left the title for other projects. George Wilson did many of the outstanding painted covers as strip artist Alden McWilliams finished out the run, ending with issue #61 in March of 1979. Surprisingly, Alberto never saw an episode of the television show, but used stills for reference that the editors provided, which might explain the flames shooting out of the Enterprise engines on some of the pages! As the first of many **Star Trek** related comics to be published by different companies over the years, this definitive version is still a favourite to Gene Roddenberry's legion of fans.

Dave Karlen

✿ ✿ ✿ ✿

STAR ROGUE
Lin Carter
1970

"A very enjoyable science fiction mystery romp..."

So, what would happen to James Bond if he was immortal, telepathic, and lived in a space empire? You'd have Saul Everest of Citadel! This is fun quick book that runs through a few days in the life of Saul when he finds some odd anomalies out on the Galactic Rim. Could this be an invasion from another galaxy? Saul comes out of retirement to investigate and the game's afoot. This book was published in 1970 and Lin Carter's predictions for the way folks in the future would live are surprisingly accurate. Phones you carry in your pocket? Check! Cameras everywhere? Check! Computers you can talk to? Check! Vehicles that have computers and can drive themselves? Check! Houses that have computers so you can tell them to lock up, unlock, change the temperature, or feed the dog? Check, Check, Check & Check! Super rich people who have their own planetoids and want to run the universe? Coming soon! At 180 pages, *Star Rogue* is a very enjoyable science fiction mystery romp. Well worth checking out!

Penny Tesarek

✿ ✿ ✿ ✿

STARTIDE RISING
David Brin
1983

"Plot twists that always keep you guessing..."

In this future, humans have begun genetically modifying (i.e., uplifting) dolphins and chimpanzees so they can be full citizens, with chimps speaking English and fins whistling haikus. Out in the universe are all these ETs that have been uplifting for billions of years because the uplifting Patron species gets to make slaves (oops, Clients) out of the uplifted species for a set number of millennia. Streaker is the first Earth starship built for a primarily Dolphin crew, with 1 Chimpanzee and several Humans to keep an eye on things. Streaker found something out there. The ETs are willing to go to war with Earth and the 5 galaxies to get their hands (or tentacles) (or beaks) on it. *Startide Rising* absolutely deserved its Hugo and Nebula awards. This book creates a future with the Earthlings as the new underdogs of the Universe. Earthlings are a wolfing race that evolved on their own instead of having their evolution guided like a bonsai, and the ETs are not happy about it. This book does a great job showing what happens when your overlords can bend your species as they choose and also what happens when the fuddy-duddies of the Universe have to contend with a species that invented star travel on their own vs just using a billion-year-old design from the Galactic Library. At 460 pages, you might be surprised at what a quick read it is – detailed characters, incredibly distinct types of aliens, battles, love stories, rotating chapter narration, plot twists that always keep you guessing, and just great science fiction. How will the Earthlings evade the attackers and keep from being crushed by the better armed ETs? Let's find out!

Penny Tesarek

✿ ✿ ✿ ✿ ✿

STOCHASTIC MAN
Robert Silverberg
1975

"Uses the concept of alternate realities and parallel universes in a pretty cool way..."

Silverberg always seems to find a way to provide a good ol' fashioned science fiction yarn and doesn't forget to add the science. He's always good at playing the what-if question and then constructing a story around it, often including some intriguing concepts to ponder along the way. The story here is about a man named Lew Nichols who uses stochastic methods to accurately predict outcomes and probabilities. He is so good at it that he is recruited by a team of people dedicated to electing the next mayor of New York, with the ultimate goal of getting their charismatic man all the way to the White House. Lew soon learns of another man who is even better at predicting events though...a man who is 100%

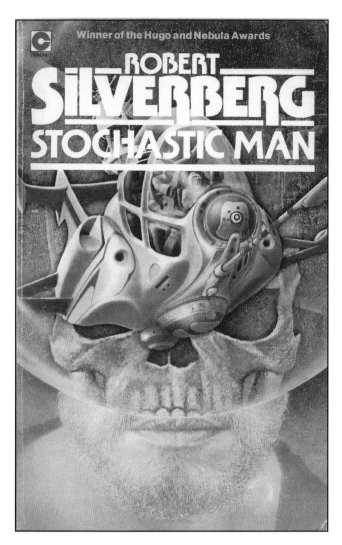

Winner of the Hugo and Nebula Awards

ROBERT SILVERBERG
STOCHASTIC MAN

accurate because he can "see" the future. Silverberg uses the concept of alternate realities and parallel universes in a pretty cool way in this novel. His what-if scenario is, "what if our timeline brushed up against a parallel universe's timeline so we could "see" what's happening over there? Only that other timeline is flowing in the reverse direction..." So, when we see into that other life, we are seeing what is still to come in our own lives. A lot of questions arise in Lew's mind, including the inevitable questions of time paradox and what happens when one witnesses their own death, but Silverberg handles them deftly. Ultimately, he explores the idea of prediction leading to predestination vs. any sort of free will to change our own paths. Intriguing concepts to be sure. This novel was written and published in the early 1970's and was nominated for a number of awards including the Nebula, Campbell, Hugo, and Locus SF awards. The plot takes place in the late 1990's, but just as Silverberg doesn't forget about the science, he also doesn't forget about the story and the characters. Curiously, for a novel about accurate predictions of the future, his own view of what life would be like in the late 1990's was way off. It's easy to look back from our vantage point now and smirk but much of what Silverberg postulated is similar from book to book and in common with other science fiction authors from that time.
Benjamin Thomas

✿ ✿ ✿ ✿

STORM OVER WARLOCK
Andre Norton
1960

"A coming-of-age novel..."

Shann Lantee, a poor and uneducated young man, feels fortunate to have achieved his goal of being included on a survey team of Terrans seeking out new planets to colonize. Unfortunately, here on the planet of Warlock, the team's survey camp has been attacked and all but destroyed by the Throgs, an alien race of beetle-like beings that have plagued mankind's ascendancy to the stars for more than a century. Shann must not only somehow survive against the Throgs but also, along with his two pet wolverines, determine the nature of the local planetary species, known for now as the Warlockians, and carve out some sort of a future for himself. One of the first novels to appear under Alice Mary Norton's pseudonym, Andre Norton, it also begins the "Forerunner" series which features a vanished

---

STOCHASTIC MAN
In case you were wondering - "Stochastic is having a random probability distribution or pattern that may be analysed statistically but may not be predicted precisely." Glad to have cleared that up. Pictured is the UK Coronet edition from 1981 with an illustration by Jim Burns. Burns' career started in 1973 and he is still going strong.

"A deft blend of the oldest of magicks in a
dragon, and the newest of sorceries in computers ...
I thoroughly enjoyed it." —Anne McCaffrey

Tea with the Black Dragon

By R. A. MacAvoy
author of Damiano

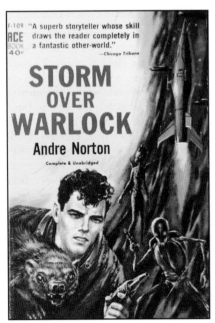

F-109
ACE
BOOK
40¢

"A superb storyteller whose skill
draws the reader completely in
a fantastic other-world."
—Chicago Tribune

STORM OVER WARLOCK

Andre Norton

Complete & Unabridged

alien race whose power was incomprehensible if the artifacts left behind are any indication. The series also loosely ties in with other Andre Norton series, most notably in the description of the "witches" found on the planet Warlock. The novel is fairly typical of an Andre Norton yarn. We have a protagonist with a less-than-ideal background, traveling across the wilderness in a largely solo affair, to ultimately surprise everyone, including himself, with a profound contribution. The aliens encountered along the way are well-developed and unique, a hallmark of Norton's work. There is plenty of adventure along the way, but also a lot of introspection from Shann. Along his journey, he discovers another Terran survivor, a survey team officer who begins by taking Shann for granted but who ultimately recognizes Shann's grit and wisdom. It's sort of a coming-of-age novel, which is also not surprising given the majority of the author's output as well as her origins as a young-adult writer. An interesting tale that pulls me toward reading more from the prolific Andre Norton.

Benjamin Thomas

is another science fiction mystery novel, beginning with an SOS to Martha Macnamara from her daughter Liz, the computer programmer. Martha hops on a plane from New York to California to lend a hand. Once she arrives, there is no sign of Liz! Horrors!! Martha begins looking for her daughter and strikes up a friendship with a long-term resident of her hotel – the mysterious Mayland Long. Martha as a heroine trying to save her daughter is so different from anyone in the Dashiell Hammett stylings. She is outgoing, open and in no way hardboiled. Mayland turns out to be a Chinese dragon in human disguise who finds that Martha is his soulmate. Mayland joins forces with Martha to search amongst the tech community and Stanford University to get to the bottom of the problem and find kidnapped Liz before she is murdered. This slim book (166 pages) keeps moving along while dropping in quite a bit about computers, California, and Chinese mythology. Enjoy!

Penny Tesarek

TEA WITH THE BLACK DRAGON
R. A. MacAvoy
1983

"About computers, California, and Chinese mythology..."

MacAvoy's debut novel was nominated for the Nebula Award, the Hugo Award and the Locus Award. She ended up winning the John W. Campbell Award for Best New Writer. Unlike every other book I am reviewing for this magazine, I had only read it once before rereading it for this review (I've read all the other ones 5-20 times before....). It was a fun book and there it was on the shelf, so what the hay, let's add it in! This

UNKNOWN WORLDS OF SCIENCE FICTION
7 issues
1975-76
Curtis Magazines

"Daring approaches and choices..."

A gloriously eclectic, intelligent, uneven and at times slap-dash, anthology comic from Curtis (owners of Marvel Comics), edited by Roy Thomas who had been instrumental in the success of the **Conan** colour comic and its mature audiences **Savage Sword of Conan** magazine. In some ways this was an attempt to replicate the **Savage Sword of Conan** formula, by being 64-pages in black and white, magazine size and adapting

TEA WITH THE BLACK DRAGON Pauline Ellison was the UK born artist behind this humorous illustration.

UNKNOWN WORLDS OF SCIENCE FICTION ISSUE 1 - ORIGINAL ART Compare the original art by Freas with the published version on page 71.

STORM OVER WARLOCK Comics fans in possession of Hulk 180 will be dismayed to know that the first appearance of the iconic Wolverine was actually on this cover painted by Ed Emshwiller.

MARVEL COMICS AMBITIOUS YET DOOMED SF COMIC

I've reviewed the run of UNKNOWN WORLDS OF SCIENCE FICTION on the previous page, so will utilise this factoid to showcase some of the excellent visuals on the cover and internals.

ISSUE TWO - Mike Kaulta recreates the famous photo of marines raising an American flag on Mount Suribachi. It represents the story 'War Toy' about a combat robot who develops emotions.

ISSUE ONE - As mentioned on the previous page. this cover was repainted from Kelly Freas' original to make the couple more realistic.

ISSUE FOUR - Frank Brunner provided a liberal interpretation of A E Van Vogt's short story 'The Enchanted Village' which is one of the run's best stories.

ISSUE FIVE - image credited to Puigdomenech. which I believe to be Sebastia Boada whose work was seen on the covers of Skywald horror comics and on German 'heftroman' fiction mags.

ISSUE SIX - Brunner provides another 'pulped to the max' image for a much more considered story.

ALEX NINO ART for 'Repent Harlequin Said the Ticktockman' and 'Behold the Man' which show his stunning and wild sense of design.

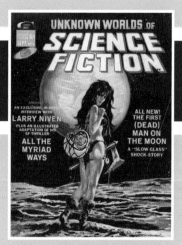

fiction stories from names beyond the field of comics. There were some daring approaches and choices, highlights being Alex Nino's anarchic art for an adaptation of Harlan Ellison's 'Repent Harlequin Said the Ticktockman', and then 'Behold the Man' by Michael Moorcock which many would consider blasphemous, especially in 1975. Artists perhaps more associated with the undergrounds or Warrens rather than Marvel were present, notably Richard Corben and Bruce Jones, although I believe they were reprints from the small-press comics. The Jones material was whimsical and bordering on pretentious, but much more affecting and sincere than any original material in the Curtis magazine range. Being Curtis/Marvel, all this boundary pushing would only be tolerated if the bottom line showed a profit. The warnings as to this commercial priority were present in issue one, when it was insisted that the legendary Kelly Freas, who had been commissioned to produce a cover illustrating the inside adaptation of *The Day of the Triffids*, paint the triffids as bug-eyed-monsters with laser-rifles emerging from a flying saucer. To add insult to injury, there was a subsequent in-house repainting of the young couple witnessing the invasion. When the sales numbers remained at break-even, despite being critically acclaimed, the mag was shut down by the money-men. After six issues, a large 'special' gathering up all the unused itinerary was published and was possibly the best issue of all. This title requires a reprint or a compilation of the best, and I think stands against the best of English-language SF comics.
Justin Marriott

✻ ✻ ✻ ✻

VALERIAN AND LAURELINE 1: THE CITY OF THE SHIFTING WATERS
Written by Christin
Art by Mezieres
1968

"Equal appeal to children and adults..."

Valerian and Laureline are the titular characters in a long-running space-opera comic strip which first appeared in French-language comics anthology **Pilote** in 1968 and has since been collected into graphic novels which are still in print to this day. It has been influential beyond the realms of comic books, recently made into a live-action film and considered an influence on the look of *Star Wars*. I remember two of their strips being published in English in the late 1970s, along with reprints of **Lucky Luke** and **Lieutenant Blueberry**, at a time when **Asterix** and **Tintin** albums were phenomenally popular. None were successful enough at the time to warrant more, but starting in 2010, Cinebooks have translated the entire series into English. Valerian and Laureline are spatio-temporal agents working for the Galaxity, a benign force who protect a future Utopia from time-travelling criminals. In *City of the Shifting Waters*, the pair visit 1986 New York in pursuit of master criminal Xombul, with the city flooded and terrorised by pirates. There is so much to recommend about this book, the art from Mezieres is loose and exaggerated but feels very believable and Christin turns in a story that is inventive and difficult to predict, with humour and nuance in the characterisation. Between them they can deliver a strip which can have equal appeal to children and adults without patronising or compromising either. In terms of late 21st century SF comics, this is amongst the very best.
Justin Marriott

✻ ✻ ✻ ✻ ✻

WAY STATION
Clifford D. Simak
1963

"How will the government deal with finding out the aliens are already here and have been for 100 years?"

I've always regretted that I never met Mr. Simak, since he was a reporter for the newspaper here in Minneapolis and lived fairly close by. I unleashed a dragon by buying Simak's copy of September 1940's **Unknown** signed by Robert Heinlein at Minicon (Minnesota's Science Fiction Convention). This was the first pulp magazine in our house, and, like an introductory taste of crack, it unlocked a pulp magazine collecting addiction in my husband that continues to this day.... *Way Station* is set in the back country hills of Wisconsin and the first two pages grab you and don't let go. It begins in 1863 with the US Civil War and one of the Union soldiers who survives that war, Enoch Wallace. Enoch returned home to work on the farm, is visited by an alien who wants to give him a job as a caretaker for interstellar travellers, and then runs the Way Station in his house for the next 100 years until the CIA notices that he's apparently immortal. Problems arise and Enoch needs to

VALERIAN AND LAURELINE: CITY OF THE SHIFTING WATERS Sequence from the Cinebooks English translation of an early Valerian and Laureline adventure, which first ran in French Bande Desinee title PILOTE in 1968. Having transported into a crumbling Statue of Liberty, which promptly collapses, time-cop Valerian is pursued by pirates across a flooded 1987 version of New York.

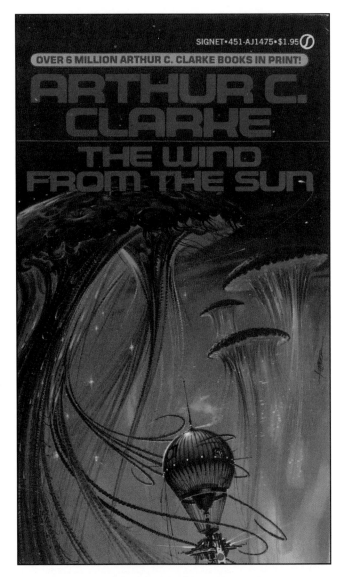

decide who he will stand with – the Earth or Galactic Central? This book just introduces concepts hither and yon. What happens when the majority of your contact is with a variety of aliens who arrive in your matter transformer, stay a few hours, and are then sent on to their next station? How can you keep up with a changing world when you don't change? How will the government deal with finding out the aliens are already here and have been for 100 years? This Hugo Award winner is one of my favourite books of all time. I reread it every year or two. You should read it too.

Penny Tesarek

THE WIND FROM THE SUN
Arthur C. Clarke
1972

"His imagination was wild, but firmly kept in restraints..."

When I was growing up, the Big Three SF authors were Robert Heinlein, Isaac Asimov and Arthur C. Clarke, Clarke being the lone Englishman. His stories were always gripping yarns, distinguishable from the others because his were solidly based in fact. He put his emphasis on "science" in "science fiction", and they had that ring of authenticity. His imagination was wild, but firmly kept in restraints. His most famous story is, of course, *2001 A Space Odyssey* (mostly because of the film, naturally), but this book is a collection of all his short stories from the same period, the Sixties. They range from spaceships powered by the 'Solar Wind' (hence the title) to the first balloon to Jupiter. Characterization is not his strong suit, so you won't really feel like you know the people in these stories – but they are all utterly convincing. Is that a Yeti or Mount Everest? Well, a cripple makes the climb using an anti-gravity device and runs into trouble, so check it out ('The Cruel Sky'). Can you kill someone with a telescope (other than bashing them over the head with it)? Read 'Light of Darkness'. And if you just want a fun story with an unexpected and malicious ending, then there's 'Reunion'. Delightful tales, every one of them.

John Peel

THE WIND FROM THE SUN
1982 edition with a Paul Alexander painting of the final story in the collection, A Meeting With Medusa, in which intrepid explorers travel through the atmosphere of Jupiter in a balloon.

74

COLLECT ALL THREE ISSUES OF THE PAPERBACK FANTASTIC

SCIENCE FICTION!

OUT NOW!

Reviews include Adam Strange, Adventures of Luther Arkwright, Alas Babylon, Armageddon 2419 AD, Atomic Knights, Barbarella, Bones of the Earth, Callahan's Crosstime Saloon, A Canticle for Leibowitz, Collision Course, The Day the Martians Came, Deathlok the Demolisher, The Destruction of the Temple, Dying of the Light, Essential Ellison, A Fighting Man of Mars, Flash Gordon, Fleshpots of Sansato, Footprints of Thunder, Frozen Hell, Gladiator-at-Law, The Glory That Was and more!

FANTASY!

MAY 2022

Reviews include Elric, Red Sonja, Kane, Bran Mak Morn, Cormac Mac Art, Fafrhrd & Gray Mouser, The Sword of Morningstar, Whetted Bronze, Brak the Barbarian, Kyrik, Wheel of Time, Brunner the Bounty Hunter, Savage Sword of Conan, Knight of Swords, Lord Foul's Bane, Volkhavaar, Spell of Seven, The Fantastic Swordsman, Blade, Slaine, Swords of Heaven, Flowers of Hell, Tales of Science and Sorcery, Nemesis the Warlock, Mythago Wood, Solomon Kane, Tarzan and more!

HORROR!

JUNE 2022

Reviews include The Ants, The Apocalypse, Books of Blood, Children of the Night, The Conjurers, The Degenerates, Devil Daddy, The Devil in the Atlas, Draco the Dragon Man, The Evil Under the Water, Headhunter, Homunculus, Killer Crabs, An Odour of Decay, Manstopper, Nightshades and Damnations, The Offspring, Sabat, The Saxonbury Machine, The Slime Beast, Tapping the Vein, Twisted Tales, Two Thousand Maniacs, Village of Blood, Whispers, The Wrath and more!